12-14-14

Claire,

Thank [illegible]r

the time you spent proofreading my book. It was a blessing. May God continue to strengthen you day by day.

Annette Whitmire

MW00940712

If Your Mountain Won't Move, Climb It!

Annette Whitmire

Copyright © 2014 Annette Whitmire.

All rights reserved. No part of this book may be used or reproduced by any means, graphic, electronic, or mechanical, including photocopying, recording, taping or by any information storage retrieval system without the written permission of the publisher except in the case of brief quotations embodied in critical articles and reviews.

Scripture taken from the King James Version of the Bible.

Scriptures taken from the Holy Bible, New International Version®, NIV®. Copyright © 1973, 1978, 1984, 2011 by Biblica, Inc.™ Used by permission of Zondervan. All rights reserved worldwide. www.zondervan.com The "NIV" and "New International Version" are trademarks registered in the United States Patent and Trademark Office by Biblica, Inc.™ All rights reserved.

WestBow Press books may be ordered through booksellers or by contacting:

WestBow Press
A Division of Thomas Nelson & Zondervan
1663 Liberty Drive
Bloomington, IN 47403
www.westbowpress.com
1 (866) 928-1240

Because of the dynamic nature of the Internet, any web addresses or links contained in this book may have changed since publication and may no longer be valid. The views expressed in this work are solely those of the author and do not necessarily reflect the views of the publisher, and the publisher hereby disclaims any responsibility for them.

Any people depicted in stock imagery provided by Thinkstock are models, and such images are being used for illustrative purposes only.
Certain stock imagery © Thinkstock.

ISBN: 978-1-4908-4553-1 (sc)
ISBN: 978-1-4908-4554-8 (e)

Library of Congress Control Number: 2014913080

Printed in the United States of America.

WestBow Press rev. date: 10/1/2014

CONTENTS

DEDICATION

It is so amazing how God puts the right people into our lives at just the right time. I have been alive now for fifty-seven years, and twenty-nine of them have been in full time ministry. I cannot begin to count how many Aarons and Hurs God has given me to help hold up my arms when I just could not do it any longer. Most of all, it has been those faithful family and friends who have surrounded me with encouragement these past eleven years since my diagnosis of cancer, that have been such a lifeline for me. There are too many to name, and I think about the verse in John 21:25 that says, "Jesus did many other things as well. If every one of them were written down, I suppose that even the whole world would not have room for the books that would be written." I feel the same way. I would fill another book or two just naming the people who have stood by me during the most trying times of my life. It is during the worst times of your life that you will get to see the true colors of the people who say they care for you. You know who you are. Thank you for faithfully praying for me and continuing to believe God for a miracle in my life. Many, many, thanks to all of my proofreaders who have painfully read my book. Then they had to reread it again because I kept changing things. I never realized the importance of commas, or that you don't have to start every sentence with "but," "so," or "and." I do now.

Thank you to all my family. I thank God for my husband, my children, my daughter-in-laws, and my beautiful grandchildren. What a blessing they have been in my life. Despite all my mistakes they turned out pretty well. I think family was one of God's best ideas.

There is one person I especially want to thank. I have known her my entire life. Although I cannot remember the first time we met, she was there for me right from the minute I was born. Through the years she became my rock.

Although she did not own a cell phone, most anytime I called her, she would be there for me, day or night. I could always count on her to tell me the truth. At times she did not have the best way of saying what she needed to say, but she said it from her heart. If I had a disagreement with my husband she would say, "Now Annette, I think you are wrong." Ouch! But I loved the times she would say, "Now Annette, I think you are right, but just ask God to help you. You have to let some things go." She was right. She was my biggest fan when I preached, and my mightiest prayer warrior. When it was time for God to take her home at age ninety-three, a piece of me went with her, and I miss her so much. With a heart full of gratitude for giving me life, I dedicate this book to my mom. She would have been so proud of me. Thank you mom for bringing me up to love and serve Jesus, regardless of how strict you were. You are the best, and I am sure you are having a wonderful time in heaven.

Most of all thank you to my Lord and Savior, Jesus Christ, who has been so faithful to me.

It is only by the grace of God that He has allowed me to accomplish this. I honestly do not know what the future holds, but I sure do know who holds my future.

~ Annette Whitmire ~

We Will Meet Again

God gave to me a mother
Who was made by His design.
And placed into our family
Just for a little time.

For though her years seemed many
They quickly passed away.
And oh what I would give
To have just one more day.

Just to say a last goodbye
Would only take a minute.
My life will never be the same
Without my mother in it.

So we must live each day,
As if it was our last.
For all our days are numbered.
And life goes by so fast.

Live each day with no regrets
And most importantly,
Make sure you are prepared
To face eternity.

Take time to make things right.
And do not hesitate.
Don't wait until tomorrow,
For tomorrow may be too late.

So Mom we'll see you soon.
Although we don't know when.
For when He calls our name,
We'll see you once again.

Annette Whitmire

Introduction

"I've learned that everyone wants
to live on top of the mountain,
but all the happiness and growth
occurs while you're climbing it."[1]

~ Author unknown ~

Have you ever had an extremely difficult day? I think we are all nodding our heads yes. There are days that are bad, and then there are days that are really bad. We all have had our share of troublesome times, but usually a good night's sleep can correct a lot of situations and readjust our frayed emotions from the day before. Ever have a day like that?

What has been the worst day of your life? The worst day of my life was not the day I discovered I had cancer. For me the worst day of my life was "the morning after." The morning you wake up and hope yesterday was just a bad dream, but then you realize it wasn't. I did not say it as poetically as Job did, but I felt the same way. Job 10:18 says, "Why then did you bring me out of the womb? I wish I had died before any eye saw me."

Life is not always easy. In fact, for some of us it is just plain hard. And to add to that, it sometimes feels downright unfair. Ever felt like that? One morning during one of my hospital stays, my oncologist, Dr. Ravi Vig, cheerfully walked into my hospital room and stood at the foot of my bed. I was a bit down because of a "minor setback" I was experiencing. I am usually a pretty positive person, but that day I was "Nancy Negative." He just smiled and said, "It's just another bump in the road. You'll get past that." It may have felt like a "bump" to him, but it felt like a mountain to me.

Just as mountains have their level of difficulty in trying to climb them, life also provides us with situations that make us feel vulnerable, and weak; they leave us with the impression that there is no hope in overcoming anything, not even a bump. You may feel your mountain is like climbing K2. K2 is the second highest mountain on the earth, also known as Godwin Austin, and it is considered the world's toughest mountain to climb. It is also called, "The Savage Mountain." It is steeper and more difficult to climb than Everest. The weather is much colder and less predictable than on Everest. For every four people who have reached the summit, one has died trying.[2] I have no desire whatsoever to even try to climb that mountain. It sounds way too risky.

What about the difficult mountains in your own life? Have you ever wanted to quit before you even started? Maybe you heard a bad report from you doctor and your prognosis was so bad that you thought, "What's the use of even trying?" I have felt like that at times. I have looked up at my mountain and have wanted to quit before I even started to try climbing it, but then I realized that I would rather die attempting to scale it, than die because I gave up and did nothing.

The title for this book was inspired by my first trip to Estes Park, Colorado. If you have never been there, it would be well worth your money and your time. My husband decided a week before we left that he needed a vacation. Unfortunately, I need at least six months to plan a major trip and my husband only needs six minutes and a few outfits. It basically takes him thirty minutes to pack. It takes me thirty days! Just ask him. A week is definitely pushing it. Men and women are so different in so many ways, and packing for a trip is one major difference. Men just pull out things from their closet and randomly stuff them into their suitcase. Then they enthusiastically announce, to your annoyance, that they are ready to go, when you have not even started. Women, on the other hand, have to try on every outfit, making sure everything matches, and most importantly fits! Then they neatly lay everything in their suitcases, usually between plastic bags, so their clothes do not get wrinkled. Note the plural of suitcase. Did I mention packing snacks, getting drinks for the cooler, putting clean sheets on all the beds, making sure all the laundry is done, the house cleaned and picked up, and if you have small children, packing their suitcases too? No wonder men are ready first!

Our first choice for vacation was going to be Prince Edward Island, a small but beautiful piece of land on Canada's eastern coast. Our inspiration came from my teenage daughter's love for "Anne of Green Gables," a family favorite with the women in our house. We were so excited to visit every spot Meghan Follows, the actress who played Anne, was filmed. But after some debate over the cost of airfare, renting a vehicle, and only having a week to plan it, we opted for our second choice, Colorado. My daughter, a self-made photographer, thought the mountains would be a good place to practice her skills in photography. So we packed (me in record time) and got into our faithful Suburban, which took us through the boring state of Kansas (sorry Dorothy) to the beautiful state of Colorado. And the mountains exceeded our expectations. They were breathtaking, literally speaking in more ways than one, due to the high altitude. Actually, my eighteen-year- old daughter passed out at a local restaurant within the first twenty-four hours of getting to Colorado. If you can get past the altitude sickness, then you are in for the view of your life!

As I focused on those majestic mountains, the Bible verse in Mark 11:23 immediately came to my mind, "Truly I tell you, if anyone says to this mountain, 'Go, throw yourself into the sea,' and does not doubt in their heart but believes that what they say will happen, it will be done for them." I think Jesus used the word "mountain" to get across the "bigness" of a problem.

I like the questions my five year old grandson asked his mother: "How does God move mountains? Aren't they really heavy?" They sure are, and He sure can! But what if your mountain will not move or even budge? We all have mountains that block our paths at times. I have a huge one I want moved. Every day I realize how hard I want to move it, and every day I realize how hard it is to move it, or even budge it. It feels as big as the mountains I saw situated in front of me in Estes Park. But as beautiful as those mountains were at the base, I was told that the view from the top was going to be even more spectacular. As I looked at one of God's most impressive creations, I thought of my own mountain that is blocking my path and thought, "If my mountain won't move, I'll climb it." And so the title of this book came to life right before my very eyes.

I cannot say that it has not been difficult, discouraging, and dangerous at times, but the views along the way and the lessons I have learned have been amazing. I hope for the next few chapters I can walk alongside of you as you climb your mountain, by sharing with you bits and pieces of my own personal experiences, difficulties, and accomplishments. I like what a friend of mine said to me one day, not knowing how perfectly it fit with this introduction. We were sitting at my kitchen table when she looked at me and said, "We tend to look at mountains as a bad thing that Jesus has to cast into the sea, but sometimes those mountains are not troubles in our lives, but triumphs! Sometimes God does not move the mountain, but calls us to climb it and conquer it." So gather your supplies, get on your hiking shoes, and let's go mountain climbing!

CHAPTER 1

Background Check

"Let your only evaluation of worth derive from the awareness of God's love for you. All other measures leave one in a state of delusion."[3]

~ Author Unknown ~

Reputation is what the world thinks a man is; character is what he really is.[4]

~ Author Unknown ~

What is on your bucket list? I never really knew what a bucket list was, until my husband challenged our congregation to have one. Some of the things listed on his were running a triathlon, fasting on Wednesdays for our children, and going elk hunting in Colorado. One of mine was writing a book. What dream has God placed inside your heart? Have you ever felt your heart pounding when you thought of that dream?

We all need dreams and bucket lists to motivate us. Sometimes we may be afraid to share our dreams, fearful of what others may think of us. Joseph was a dreamer, and he was not afraid to share his dreams. In fact, he shared them with his entire family, but instead of encouraging him, they became angry with him, including his father. His brothers had so much jealousy and anger issues towards him, that it almost took them to the point of killing him. Years passed, and his cherished dreams turned into haunting nightmares. His dreams were forgotten by everyone, everyone that is, except God. I wonder if Joseph gave up on his dreams during all those difficult and silent years. I wonder if they were so real to him, that he held on to them, even though he could not understand why they were not being fulfilled. Hold on to your dreams, even though they are not happening now. Hold on to your dreams even if you cannot understand how they will materialize.

My husband is a gift giver. He usually gives me something for every holiday, even if it is just a card. But sometimes he gives me a gift for no reason, and those are the best gifts to receive. I was in the hospital once for a few weeks, and he brought a small gift bag into my room. I opened it up, and it has become one of my favorite gifts, my inspiration when I feel like giving up. It is a little wall hanging that simply says, "Never give up on your dreams." I have it sitting by my computer as I try to compose this book, so please do not ever give up on your dreams.

God's timing is always the right timing. For years I wanted to write a book, but what has really motivated me to do it was a diagnosis of cancer. This made me put everything into perspective. I realize that my days are numbered, and I had better start checking off my bucket list.

My decision to start this book-writing journey was confirmed by several incidents. I would first like to go back to a new friend I made in the airport. It happened while I was waiting for one of my connecting flights on a trip back east to visit my family in Pennsylvania. I did not realize it, but some "stranger" was looking over my shoulder reading the beginnings of this very book. She asked me, "Are you a writer?" I laughed. Out loud, I think. And for one split second I pretended I was. Then I thought about that and realized that we do not have to be an author of a book to feel important. We all are somebody special in God's eyes, and we all have a story to tell that will bless someone else.

I was reading about that in one of the magazines the Assemblies of God sends out for Women's Ministries. It encouraged us to realize that God has given each one of us a story to tell. We all are unique. Our lives are like snowflakes. No two are exactly alike. Though some of your lives are very fragile, telling your story could have a strong influence on those you tell it to, whether you believe it will or not. Your story has the potential to help someone in a way my story cannot. Each of us can connect emotionally in different ways to different people. You are only one chapter in God's big story book, but a very important chapter. Without it, the book is not complete.[5] Did you know you can give hope to someone else? Isn't that what the Bible is all about? When we read stories of characters in the Bible who endured tragedy and pain, it not only gives us hope, but the perspective and courage to keep going. Keep climbing! You might say, "I have such a sinful past. How can God use me?"

Did you ever look at the women who were listed in Jesus' genealogy? The first woman was Tamar, who was Jacob's grand-daughter. She tricked her father-in-law, Judah, into thinking she was a harlot, and in the process became pregnant with her father-in-law's children.

Twins, no less! That's just the first woman in His genealogy. Her story is in Genesis 38. Then there was Rahab, a Canaanite woman. Remember, the Canaanites were the enemies of God's people, rivals who fought the Israelites every step of the way into the Promised Land. She not only was a gentile, she was a real harlot by profession! You can read her story in Joshua 2. Next there was Ruth. I love the story of Ruth. She actually was a good woman, but the only problem was that she was a Moabite woman. Who were the Moabites? They were the race that resulted from the union of Lot (Abrahams' nephew) and his oldest daughter. The Jews were forbidden to marry anyone who was not a Jew, and Moabites were considered to be the worst of all gentiles. Psalm 108 calls Moab God's washbasin. That is not a very nice compliment! You can read the story of Ruth in four thought-provoking chapters. Then there was Bathsheba. She may have been a victim, but she was a gentile woman who slept with King David, after he watched her taking a bath! And that is only part of their story. I am sure if they told us their whole story, it might make us blush.

The Bible is listed as the number one book ever written, with four billion copies sold.[6] Not only were these women included in one of the greatest books ever written and sold, but they were included in Jesus' genealogy. If these women's stories could make it into one of the greatest books in history, be listed in one the most important genealogies, and have such an impact on us today, I know you can share your story with someone and positively influence their life.

I hope I will give you the motivation you need to do what is on your bucket list, especially if it is writing a book. This is one thing I always wanted to do, but never thought I could, and now I am struggling every day trying to do it. In the past two years I watched three of my friends write a book and each bring a copy of their books to me. They have no idea how much they silently encouraged me to do this. And that is why I love that verse in Philippians 4:13 which says, "I can do all this (*even writing a book*) through Him who gives me strength." This is such a good verse for all of us, and one that we need to speak out every day of our lives.

My oldest son is a police officer. When he pulls someone over he does a quick type of background check to see if that person has committed any prior crimes he should be aware of, or if there are any warrants out for their arrest. I know how important a background check is today when you are applying for a job, especially one related to children. We have background checks for all nursery workers and teachers in our church, if they are working with children under the age of eighteen.

So here is a little "background check" on me, since some of you have no idea who I am. And for those who do, here is a little more you might not have known. The only close to illegal thing I did was getting a warning ticket for going thirty-five mph in a twenty-five mph zone. I was actually late going to church, but I figured the officer would never buy that one! I really did not think I was going that fast but I am sure that is a typical response of a lot of people who get stopped. How could I be speeding? My kids describe me as "Grandma" when I drive. When the officer pulled me over he said, "Do you know why I stopped you?" I honestly did not think I was speeding so I said, "No." He said, "You were going ten miles over the speed limit!" I said, "I really did not realize it. Honestly." Maybe I won by not getting a speeding ticket but that was my first and only warning ticket.

The other situation that I vaguely remember is when I knocked over someone's mailbox with my car, totally by accident. Unfortunately, it was on the street we lived on, which for all practical purposes made us neighbors. I turned around to spank one of my kids while driving to work and heard an unwelcomed banging noise. As I quickly turned my eyes back to where they should have been in the first place, I watched the right front bumper of my Volvo making contact with my neighbor's mailbox. I actually left the scene of the crime because I would have been late for work if I stopped. After work, I went to my neighbors to confess that I was the one who did it. I slowly walked up the sidewalk as they were repairing their "hit and run" mailbox. I felt terrible, but they were very gracious. We did not text and drive, back in the day; we did what they would now call, "spank and drive." And my boys never let me forget that one till this very day.

I will try to compress fifty-seven years into a few paragraphs for now and then give you the specifics in the next chapter. I was actually called to the ministry when I was around eight or nine years old. Never underestimate the salvation or call of a child. I think of the amazing story of Samuel in the Bible. I Samuel 3:10 says, "The Lord came and stood there, calling as at the other times, 'Samuel! Samuel!' Then Samuel said, 'Speak, for your servant is listening.'" God spoke to me many times during my "growing up years." Not audibly like Samuel heard, but heart to heart all the way through to my adult life.

After high school I attended Valley Forge Christian College, in Phoenixville, Pennsylvania, where God began preparing me for ministry. Following Bible College I attended Burge School of Nursing in Springfield, Missouri, where I received my registered nurse's degree. I met my husband during my junior year in September and married him the following July. Two years and two children later, we entered the world of ministry. I have been a pastor's wife for twenty-nine years, and I am still learning to trust God every day.

God keeps telling me I have a story to tell and so does a man in our church named Len Miles. He always asks me, "When are you going to write your book?" Thanks Len for the encouragement! I have decided that even if just one person gets blessed by this book, it will be worth it because God cares about individuals. It reminds me of the story of the Good Shepherd. He left ninety-nine of his flock to help the one sheep who was lost and struggling. This book is for that one person who is lost or struggling to make sense out of the mountain that is blocking their path. Hold on sister or brother, and keep climbing!

CHAPTER 2

WHO AM I AND WHY AM I HERE?

"Your character is far more important than your past or your future; it's who you are that matters, not what you've done or will do."[7]

~ Anonymous ~

I was born and raised in New York City on 12th Street and First Avenue, otherwise known as the Lower East Side of Manhattan. I was the last of three children, or "the baby," as my siblings and husband referred to me. Still do. My mom had me later in life, and she made sure everyone knew I was not an accident or "a change of life baby," as they called it back then. I have an older sister in heaven who literally gave her life for me. About a year before I was born, my mom had a miscarriage, a baby girl. If she had been born, I would not be here. I am looking forward to meeting her in heaven someday. On my good days I thank her for life, and on the bad days I blame her.

We lived on the second floor of a four-story apartment building. It was a small two-bedroom, roach-infested, no air conditioner, and no dishwasher apartment. Because I was the youngest, it was also a no-bedroom-for-me apartment. Actually, my bedroom consisted of a single sized, pull out, Castro Convertible bed that transformed into an extra sofa during the daytime hours. It was located in the living room—a couch by day and a bed by night. It kind of reminded me of the children of Israel, in a way. We also had a compact living room table that converted from a coffee table into a dining room table by lifting it up or pushing it down. It reminded me of those toys my kids played with years ago, "Transformers, more than meets the eye." It even had leaves that folded out to make it larger when company came to eat. It really was a cool table. It is funny the things you remember and the things you choose not to remember. Our kitchen tub doubled as our kitchen counter. There was a thick piece of plywood that covered our bathtub, so you did not have the privilege of taking a bath every day, because it was too much trouble to get everything off of it. Mom probably made that rule. On the non-bath days, you sponged off in the kitchen sink. Dad also shaved there. That is why mom never put any dishes in the sink. She used a small basin she placed next to the sink to wash them in. On the days you wanted to bathe, you locked the front door, located in the kitchen, and fastened the louver door between the kitchen and the living room.

Mom was the guard that kept intruders from entering the kitchen during bath time.

My sister Rosemarie, eighteen years my elder, was married and gone by the time I was one year old. She was more like a second mother to me. My brother, Junior, that is what I called him; and I do not think he liked it as an adult, was fourteen years older than me. He had the only other bedroom, which was more like a big closet. We had a ringer washer and had two options to dry our clothes depending on the season. In the summer we would hang our clothes on the clothesline located outside our kitchen window for the whole neighborhood to see, and in the winter we would place them on radiators that were strategically placed in each room, which were also our sole source of heat. Either way, our clothes turned out stiff, and the towels felt like you were using sandpaper to dry yourself off after your bath.

Our apartment was sandwiched in with my mom's side of the family. My Aunt Connie, Uncle Jimmy, and my cousin Frank Guella, lived in an apartment on the first floor of our building. We lived on the second floor. The Fallettas, which included Aunt Betty, Grandma Anna, and Uncle Sal, all lived on the third floor. We had family directly below and directly above us. Aunt Frances and Uncle Frank Cacciatore were the smart ones who chose to live down the street with my cousin James, putting a little distance between them and the rest of the family. Some of my dad's relatives lived within several city blocks. In case you could not figure it out, we were a close Italian family. The names ending in vowels should have given it away.

Down the street and around the corner there was a vegetable stand where we had fresh produce. It was like having a farmer's market every day. My mother loved to tell the "Veggie Tales" story about my brother. He was a very energetic child. I think if he were a child growing up today he probably would have been placed on Ritalin, but instead he got some pretty good spankings, which worked fairly well without all the bad side effects. My brother was always getting into trouble. Back in the day, the fruits and vegetable were all stacked neatly in a beautiful looking pyramid. The first thing my brother would do was run to one of those pyramids, and before my mom could stop him, he would quickly remove the bottom fruit or vegetable so he could watch all the others tumble down on the ground. When the merchant would see my mom and brother come in, it did not matter if it was her turn or not, they would say, "Serve this woman first!" Wondering how he turned out? He has been married for forty three years and has become a great self-made, successful businessman. And he is very well behaved in the produce department.

On that same street there was a butcher where we got fresh meat. And I mean fresh. Once, my brother talked my mother into letting him have a cute baby chick for a pet. Obviously it grew into a mama chicken. Imagine a full grown chicken running around a small New York City apartment. I cannot believe she let him have one. The only pet I could have was a goldfish. Talk about equal rights. Finally, she could not take it any longer. Of course, you do not eat your pet, at least not here in America, so she traded ours for a fresh, ready-to-cook one, and someone else got to eat our pet. We also had one of the best bakeries where they had delicious Italian bread and cookies, along with a wonderful pizzeria and various other stores for your convenience, all in about a city block or two.

Besides going shopping with my mom, I remember the times when I stood on the corner with her, handing out gospel tracts. That was one of my fondest memories I have of my mom. She was not ashamed of Jesus or His gospel. I think she knew people were more likely to take a pamphlet from a little Italian "bambina" than a short Italian "signora."

I attended elementary school at PS 19, along with Lady Gaga, which was right across the street from the apartment building we lived in. Different years of course and I assure you that is the only thing we had in common! The only thing I got in trouble for in grade school was talking, except for this one incident. I do not know why I did it, but I remember I was in the bathroom along with another girl from my class. All of a sudden we started taking wads of toilet paper, wetting them in the sink, and then throwing them up on the ceiling. Maybe that is when they invented the "popcorn ceiling." I do not know whose idea it was, and I cannot remember the details, but I guess I was too long going to the bathroom. My accomplice left, and I was caught red handed by my teacher. I think I had to go to the principal's office and my mom came and got me. I was extremely embarrassed, but not as much as my mom. She was mad too. And I am sure I got a good spanking when I got home. Those were my rebellious elementary school years.

I was raised in a strong Christian home. My mom was a very kind and giving person, who always brought into our home those people whom no one else would ever talk to, let alone have in their homes as guests. Down the street there was an older widowed man who did not always smell the best, who was a frequent guest at our house. There was also a woman and her three children who had a lot of family issues, who came for coffee and a Bible study quite frequently. Although we did not have a lot of money, a pot of my mom's homemade soup and a loaf of fresh Italian bread would go a long way to feed a lot of hungry mouths and hearts.

Looking back now, I know there were several incidents where God spared my life. The first I mentioned was my mom's miscarriage about a year before I was born. You may not think that counts, but I do. Times were difficult and money was tight. My parents really could not afford another child, but my mom won the debate. And they were only going to have one more child. How I see it, I barely made it. Why did I live and not my sister? I just do not know but I know there is a reason for me to be here. Sometimes I question why God allowed me to live and then have to fight cancer for the rest of my life. I do not think I am going to get that one answered to my satisfaction, at least not in this lifetime.

The second incident is a bit more dramatic. We were going on a family vacation to Keswick, in Whiting, New Jersey. It was a Christian family camp, and I think it is still there today. It was mom, dad, and me as well as my sister, her husband, and my niece, who was three years younger than I. She was more like the sister I always begged for but never got. We stopped for a break on a country road to look at a view or stretch our legs. I cannot remember all the details, but I remember my dad pulling off the road and parking the car. As soon as we jumped out of our vehicle we noticed a path. Although we were warned not to run ahead, what do you think two energetic kids did who had been cooped up in their car for a few hours? We started running and heard our parents' voices fade into the distance. There were no other cars around. It looked like a deserted country road that you should not go on with or without your parents. We had no fear and lots of pent-up energy. As we were running down the path, laughing and seeing who could get there first, wherever "there" was, from out of nowhere two elderly people grabbed us as they commanded, "Children stop!" It was a man and woman. I mean they literally came out of nowhere. It was as if they were waiting for us. That freaked us out more than anything. While they were holding us, our parents were just seconds away from catching up with us. I think they were yelling for us as they were running, but when we all took in the scene that was being played out before our eyes, we all became silent. The couple told our parents to look as they pointed to what could have been a beautiful view, under different circumstances. To our horror, there was a precipice that dropped hundreds of feet to a rocky bottom. There were no signs, no fencing, and nothing that would warn you of the impending danger. We would have both literally ran off that cliff to our deaths had not this couple been there. Of course my mom grabbed me and my sister grabbed my niece, and they were scolding us, hugging us, and crying at the same time. We started crying too. Just a few seconds passed and my family turned to thank the couple, but they were gone. My brother-in-law ran down the road a ways to try to catch them. Remember they were old and my brother-in-law was young. They literally vanished into thin air. We all came to the same conclusion, they were our guardian angels, and no one can tell me otherwise. Psalm 91:11 says, "For He will command His angels concerning you to guard you in all your ways. . ." And I keep running my guardian angels ragged.

When I was twelve we moved to the country, or Brooklyn, New York. After living in "the asphalt jungle," Brooklyn was the country to us. One of the reasons we moved was because the junior high I was supposed to attend in Manhattan was, as my mom said, "full of drugs." The neighborhood was "getting bad," too. I heard my mom say that phrase many times. She wanted me to go to a Christian School in Brooklyn. I cannot believe the sacrifice my entire family made for me so I could go to a Christian school. All my aunts, uncles, and cousins followed us. The working men all had to commute back to Manhattan to go to work every day. And what was one of the biggest reasons? Me! I really did not realize the sacrifice they all made till now. The extra perk, and the other reason was my older sister and her family lived there, too. Remember, close Italian families stay together. When one moves, they all move. And they followed my sister from Brooklyn, to New Jersey, and finally to Pennsylvania.

Brooklyn was definitely the country. There were more trees, and we actually had our own 6' x 8' section of yard in the front of our four-family house, where we grew a rose bush, and a little larger plot in the back of the house where we grew tomato plants and a fig tree. The "stoop" was where we hung out and visited with the neighbors on the block as they walked by. They were either Jewish or Italian. Mom would frequently invite the neighbors over for coffee and cake, but of course her main reason was to share the gospel. I guess she knew about "Friendship Evangelism" way before they invented it. She had a strong faith, and whatever the conversation was, it would always turn to spiritual truths, whether you wanted to hear it or not. Sometimes her style of witnessing was not the best. She was pretty dogmatic about certain things, and for those she would not budge. But at least she did what God has commanded all of us to do. I do not know if there ever were any true converts, but she planted lots of seeds, and she never gave up. I guess only eternity will tell the story.

I attended New York Christian Academy, a private Christian school that my church had from seventh through tenth grade. When it closed down due to lack of funds, I attended Franklin Delano Roosevelt High School for my junior and senior years. It was a rude awakening from the Christian bubble I came out of. I remember one day we were on lock down and confined to the second floor because of racial gang wars. When we were released, I walked into what looked like a small war zone. Someone had taken a baseball bat and shattered a block of windshields in retaliation to who knows what. Probably someone looked at somebody wrong or someone stole somebody's girlfriend. That was the only time I was glad my parents could not afford a car for me.

The women in our family never learned how to drive. Since all you needed was in walking distance of your apartment, it was not really necessary. My dad was determined I would be different. He made me learn to drive, and I am forever grateful to him for that. I was the first female in the family to have a driver's license. He was pretty patient with me, except this one time. I had a fear of driving over bridges, even as a passenger, let alone a driver. One day he took me for a normal practice drive. Everything was going well, when unexpectedly I saw the sign for "The Brooklyn Bridge." I was terrified and Dad knew it. I looked at him and said, "Dad, I don't want to do this." But he firmly said, "Yes, you will." And I did. The only bad thing was I had to do it again to go back home, and he made me do that, too. I still do not like driving over bridges, but I am so glad I learned to drive.

After high school I attended Valley Forge Christian College for three years, where God confirmed His call on my life for ministry. When I completed a three year missions program, God led me to Burge School of Nursing in Springfield, Missouri, where I became a registered nurse and also obtained my MRS. degree. It was really a lot like the old television show, "Green Acres." A city girl from Manhattan meets a country boy from

Salem, Missouri, population 4,454.[8] After we both graduated, me from nursing school and my husband from Drury College, we moved back to his hometown where we resided in "The Waiting Room" for two years. He worked for Craig Distributing Company, and I was a part-time nurse and a full-time mom of two very energetic boys twenty one months apart. We were very involved with our local church youth group, but for those two years I wondered if I had married out of God's will. I knew God called me to full-time ministry, but why wasn't my husband hearing that? But over the years I have come to realize that God is never early, He is never late, but He is always on time, His time. God was training and preparing both of us, and when the time was right, God called my husband to full-time ministry. With a two-year-old and a two-month-old, it was back to Springfield, Missouri, for Chuck to attend Central Bible College and seminary while I worked full-time at Cox Medical Center as a registered nurse. Those were difficult years on one hand, but wonderful learning experiences on the other. God truly grew us up there. After two years of God's stretching and training, God opened the door for us to take a full-time position in Steelville, Missouri, where Chuck was a youth pastor for five years. Those were some of the best times in our life. Pastor Harris and his wife, Lisa, were such good mentors to both of us, more than they will ever know. When the time for us to leave there came, God opened the door for us to pastor our first church in Rolla, Missouri, where we are still today after twenty four years. God has truly blessed us with a wonderful group of people and many close friends.

This is a little of who I was and who I am. But it does not matter who you are or what training you have. It does not matter how long you are in the ministry or if you are in the ministry. When there is a mountain in *your* path, it seems to bring a different perspective to things. It is one thing to help someone through their difficult situation, encouraging them and praying through with them, but when it happens to you, it can knock the wind out of you no matter how much practice you have had with someone else.

So what is your mountain? Are you just sitting there waiting for it to move? I am not here for us to have a contest on who has the biggest mountain to climb or why some mountains will not budge. Other people can write those books. The fact is, we all have obstacles in our way. And if we do not now, we will in the future. It is not what kind of mountain we have, or how big it is, it is what are we going to do with it and what are we going to allow it to do to us. My mom would always say it will either make you bitter or better, and though we know which outcome we want, it is not always easy getting there. With God's strength you can do it. So you can stop to rest for a while, but then get up and keep climbing!

CHAPTER 3

Please Tell Me What Must I Do To Be Healed?

"You can't have healing without sickness."[9]

~ T.D. Jakes ~

If you are hoping this book is a 12-step guide on how to get healed or delivered from whatever your problem is, then stop reading it right now and go get your money back. Sorry to disappoint you. I know there are a lot of good books out there on how to claim your healing. There are books that try to tell you exactly why you are not getting whatever you are so desperately praying for and how to fix it. This book is not about that. I am writing from a different perspective. My inspiration comes from my own personal experience in battling with cancer and struggling with God to heal me the way I want Him to, using the methods I want Him to use. Do you ever struggle with that? Most of all, this book is intended to be an encouragement to help you keep on keeping on when you think you cannot do it any longer. We all need someone to help support us and tell us not to give up!

The title of this chapter may be a little familiar looking. It is a play on words and it is taken from the powerful story in Acts chapter 16 about Paul, Silas, and the Philippian jailer.

Paul and Silas were thrown into prison one day for preaching the gospel, but about midnight, in the middle of their praise and worship time, there was a supernatural earthquake. All the prison doors flew open, and the jailer was getting ready to kill himself because he thought all the prisoners had escaped. Not only did not one of the prisoners escape, it did not appear that they even tried to. Maybe they were as stunned as everyone else. The scripture does say that the prisoners were listening to this special concert. Maybe they saw a connection or maybe they were waiting for the altar call. It is so amazing that they all stayed in their cells. I do not know if they were too scared to move because of the earthquake, or God glued their feet to the ground so they would not escape, but the bottom line is they did not move. That part of the story is more supernatural to me than the earthquake. God can and will move anytime, anywhere, when He chooses, under the right circumstances, under the wrong circumstances, and always for His glory. Just as the jailer was getting ready to slice his jugular or sever his carotid, Paul screamed out, "Don't hurt yourself!" I think the jailer had to be listening too, and he had to be amazed that no one even tried to escape. So he got down on his knees and said in Acts 16:30, "Sirs, what must I do to be saved?"

So many times I have gotten down on my knees and asked God the same question, "God, what must I do to be healed?" Have you ever said that? And believe me, I have gotten many opinions from well-meaning people on how to do it or why it is not happening. Maybe you do not need to be healed, but the situation you are in has held you captive for a long time. My prison is my body. You can run away from other situations, but you cannot detach yourself from your body. That would hurt. You are attached and as they say in marriage, it is "till death do you part." Does God still heal? Absolutely! But does He heal everyone? The answer is yes and no. Hold on a minute. As a believer we all will be healed when we get our perfect body without pain or sickness in heaven someday. Oh, that's not what you were thinking? But on this earth, the answer is no. Now do not stone me for false doctrine. Let me try to clarify what I am saying.

John the Baptist, the forerunner of Jesus, His first cousin on death row, doubted who Jesus was. Imagine that. He may have doubted His power to do anything for him at that low point in his life. Probably, since nothing was happening for his release, he thought he better find out if Jesus forgot about him. He wanted to know if his cousin was for real, since it appeared that he was not getting any help from Him when he needed it the most. He sent his disciples to ask Jesus this thought-provoking question in John 7:20: "Are you really who you say you are, or is someone else coming who will get me out of this mess?" (*My translation*) I mean wait. How could he even ask such a question? We can get pretty human when we are at our lowest point, but God still loves us. John baptized Jesus and saw heaven open, and he heard God's voice audibly and saw with his human eyes the spirit descending on Jesus, however that happened. Surely that was more than enough not to doubt who Jesus was? Ever! Yet he did doubt, and Jesus did not help him. Was it because He doubted that Jesus did not save him? I don't think so. Jesus specifically said in John 7:22, "Go back and report to John what you have seen and heard: The blind receive sight, the lame walk, those who have leprosy are cleansed, the deaf hear, the dead are raised, and the good news is proclaimed to the poor." In other words He was saying, "John, you know I can do miracles of any kind. You saw me do all of them. I am for real." But here is the clincher. He said in Matthew 11:6, "Blessed is anyone who does not stumble on account of Me." The word to "fall away or stumble," depending on your translation, is "skandalizōl." It means "to cause a person to begin to distrust and desert one whom he ought to trust and obey."[10] What an appropriate word Jesus used. He knew John was doubting, and He wanted John to know, although He was not going to rescue him, He did not want him to fall away spiritually over this one situation. But this was big. John was on death row for doing the right thing, and Jesus chose not to rescue him. Why? He even said in Matthew 11:11, "Truly I tell you, among those born of women there has not risen anyone greater than John the Baptist." So why wouldn't Jesus help him at a time he needed Him the most? Because

He is God, period! Were you looking for a more theological answer? I guess we can use the cliché, "It was for God's glory!" Well, wouldn't it have been so much more awesome to see God miraculously deliver Him? Wouldn't that be so much better than people saying, "He couldn't even help His own cousin? What a shame."

What about Paul? You know, the guy who wrote most of the New Testament. Paul asked the Lord three times to take his "thorn in the flesh" away, whatever that was, and what was God's response to him in II Corinthians 12:9? "My grace is sufficient for you, for My power is made perfect in weakness." Do you ever wonder why he only asked three times? I have, because I have asked God probably a hundred times or more in eleven years to heal me. In other words God said, "No, Paul, I cannot help you by taking it away but I will help you by giving you the strength you will need to endure it." So why didn't He heal Paul? Because He is God, period! I know that might not be a good enough answer for some of you. I would rather those verses not be in the Bible unless they were a little easier to understand. I think Isaiah says it best. Isaiah 54:8-9 says, "For My thoughts are not your thoughts, neither are your ways My ways, declares the Lord. As the heavens are higher than the earth, so are My ways higher than your ways and My thoughts than your thoughts." Guess we forget that little fact. Can we just trust God because He is God? Remember He is the Creator of the heavens and earth. He is the one who flung the stars into space and He is the one who created us from the dust of the earth. Do we think He knows what He is doing? It doesn't mean we have to agree with it or even like it, but He is God!

Now before you really turn me off, this book is not intended to discourage you or make you think God does not heal, will not heal, or answer any of your prayers. Absolutely not! We continue to ask, seek, and knock until we get a yes, or we get a clear no, the rapture comes, or He takes us home. "No, not death," you say. Actually, we make death seem like our enemy, but Mr. Death must come for us to get to heaven. I loved to watch that TV series, "Touched By An Angel." Although their theology was not always quite correct, it was a pretty wholesome show to watch. You would really get into the episode until Andrew, portrayed by John Dye, the "Angel of Death," would show up. That would ruin everything. Unless your name is Enoch or Elijah, or the rapture happens, you are going to have to go by the way of the grave. Bummer! We are not going to get there in a flaming, flying, Ferrari either, and for sure not in a flaming chariot of fire. Unfortunately, as my mom would say, "None of us are going to get out of this world alive." And from what I have read, heaven is not such a bad place to go. I made my reservation for 2057. That would make me 100 years old! All joking aside, I genuinely want to receive my healing now. I know you want to be delivered now, too. My mom always said where there is life there is hope.

What are you supposed to do if you want to be healed or delivered or get whatever you need from God? What is the bottom line? If you believe the Bible and you believe God heals, and I do, keep on believing, keep on praying, keep on knocking, or pounding on heaven's door till you break it down. God still wants to do miracles in your life. He has done miracles, and He will continue to do miracles. Remember, we are only one small speck on this earth. How big does that make our brain? That's one of the reasons our thoughts don't even come close to God's thinking. I know we assume we could have done things a lot better than we think God is doing. It is so hard to understand Him at times. Believe me. I live there most of the time. Most of us have no clue how God is moving in the seven billion people that live on this earth. It is not just about America, or Missouri, or Rolla, or wherever you live. It is not just about me or you. We are self-centered to think that it is all about us. God is always working out His will in people's lives every day. What is this book about, anyway? It is how to claim your healing or whatever you desperately need from God without losing your mind or stifling how God wants to use you, if you do not get it the way you want it.

I like that song by John Waller, "While I'm Waiting." It talks about serving God while you are waiting. Just because you have cancer, or are going through a divorce, have chronic pain, lost a husband, are out of work, are being abused, are a single parent, have a child on drugs, or whatever you are suffering through, it does not mean you just sit there and wait. It does not mean you just twiddle your thumbs and tell God you will serve Him when He heals you or if He delivers you. No! You serve Him while you are waiting, and you will be amazed how God will use you. God has opened up so many opportunities for me because of my cancer that I would not have had if I did not have it. Now I am not so deranged that I am saying you have to have cancer to have these good opportunities, or if you are healthy God cannot use you as well. No, No, No! What I do want to emphasize is that in every bad situation you can always pull out something good. You should at least try to see something good. It will help you to keep your sanity and get you through it.

I want to go back to my new friend I met in the airport. I was sitting down waiting for the boarding call to sound, typing a chapter for this book on my new iPad. I was having trouble spelling the word "stifling." Ever get a brain freeze or a senior moment? Sometimes the word "the" doesn't look right to me. Anyway, the lady next to me smiled and said, "One l." At first it confused me, and then I got it. She was proofreading my book, and I did not know it. I smiled and said thanks and thought, "This is a God moment that I would not be having if I did not have cancer, because I would not be writing this book, and I probably would not be talking to this young lady." She continued and said, "I was intrigued by what you were writing. Are you an author?" After having my one second of fame, I laughed, but then proceeded to tell her my experience, which of course has God all over it. This is what I mean. Please do not let your circumstances stifle (thank you airport lady) how God wants to use you while you are climbing your mountain. Remember, our ways are not His ways by a long shot. Chris (that was the airport lady's name) if you are reading this book, thank you for giving me the opportunity to share Christ with you, and may God bless you as you find your purpose in life.

CHAPTER 4

CLIMB, CLIMB UP SUNSHINE MOUNTAIN YOU AND I!

"If all you can do is crawl,
start crawling."[11]

~ Rumi ~

Do you remember that old children's song, "Climb, climb up sunshine mountain heavenly breezes blow? Climb, climb up sunshine mountain faces all aglow?"[12] That was a fun kid's song to sing, but that is not really a good picture of what the difficult mountains in our life feel like. I wish life was that easy. Life is not always easy, and life does not always seem that fair at times. With God's help you can persevere, even if you have to crawl through your trial.

At times I felt like that was what I was doing. When I first got diagnosed with cancer, that mountain stopped me dead in my tracks. I literally thought it was going to kill me. If I had listened to Satan and his lies I would have missed out on the climb of my life. If I would have listened to the Father of Lies, I would have stayed curled up in a fetal position waiting to die. I thank God for verses like Philippians 4:13 which says, "I can do all this through Him who gives me strength." Or verses like Isaiah 40:29 which says, "He gives strength to the weary and increases the power of the weak."

I love Psalm 18:32-34. It says, "It is God who arms me with strength and keeps my way secure. He makes my feet like the feet of a deer; He causes me to stand on the heights. He trains my hands for battle; my arms can bend a bow of bronze." This last verse was written by David during one of the many times God delivered him from his father-in-law, Saul. David was going through a difficult time in his life. Saul was always trying to physically kill his son-in-law, God's future king. David had to physically climb up steep hills and mountains, trying to stay alive by distancing himself from his psychotic father-in-law. And I guarantee you it was not "Sunshine Mountain."

Another scripture of encouragement is Isaiah 40:31. It says, "But those who hope in the Lord will renew their strength. They will soar on wings like eagles; they will run and not grow weary, they will walk and not be faint." I could go on and on giving you scripture after scripture. Without the inspired, infallible, and living word of God, it would be hard to get out of bed in the morning. You may need a cup of coffee to wake you up, but I need to hear God speaking to me, and one of the ways He speaks is through His word.

Did you know it is not our job to move our mountain? That is God's job and He will accomplish that anyway He pleases. He actually can do it without our help, even though we think we know better than Him or have some great ideas to assist Him. Whatever your mountain is, whether it is financial, spiritual, physical, or emotional, God is in control. Whether it is a child, a husband, a wife, or any other situation, He can get the job done. There is one thing He does want us to do. I Peter 5:7 says it best. "Cast all your anxiety on Him because He cares for you." Please don't just sit there feeling overwhelmed. Allow Him carry your burdens so you can keep climbing, or crawl if you have to.

CHAPTER 5

THE BIG C

"At any given moment you have the power to say this is NOT how the story is going to end."[13]

~ Author unknown ~

Never in a million years would I have ever thought I would be hearing a doctor say, "You have cancer." As a student nurse I worked on the oncology floor, which, ironically, was the one floor I said I never wanted to work on. I took care of terminally ill patients, watched some of them die, and had to be in the room when the doctor told the family the dreaded news. I remember taking care of a patient one day and walking into their room the next, only to find their bed neatly made and in the raised position. And it was not because they went home. I never imagined this depressing scene would be played out in my life. Well maybe when I was ninety, but not at forty-six.

Unfortunately, we do not always have control over situations like this, which is really hard for controlling women who always like to fix things in their husband, in their children, in their friends, and in their own life. But this was one thing I knew was out of my control. Oh, you do have some control. You choose your doctor and then you can choose to take chemo, change your lifestyle, take nutritional supplements, and exercise, but God is the only one who can miraculously heal you, and that is how I wanted it. I wanted a full blown, New Testament, Holy Ghost miracle—still do. I still believe. Now this is just me of course. I just did not want to take chemo and have the doctors say they did it. Actually I just did not want to take chemo. Period! I did not want to put those strong chemicals into my body and have all those dreadful side effects. Chemo just doesn't attack your bad cells, unfortunately it kills the good cells and weakens healthy organs, not on purpose, but it has not quite been perfected yet. I also did not want people to think I had lack of faith, which some did anyway. I wanted it my way, which was a good idea. I wanted a real live miracle like Jesus said would happen if you asked Him. Doesn't that make sense and sound so much better? I thought so. But of course God has the trump card, so to speak, and He does what He wants to do, how He wants to do it, and when He wants to do it. He usually does not ask our opinion, no matter how good it may seem.

And so my biggest mountain appeared eleven years ago when my children were twenty-two, twenty, sixteen, and eight. For the past several months I had been feeling tired, to the point of being fatigued. I had recently had my yearly check-up and told my doctor that I just did not feel right. I felt exhausted. He brushed it off as me being a very active person with my family and my community. He essentially said the same thing the year before. Guess I looked too healthy. But I persisted and he set me up with a great internist. Come to find out, this physician went to school with my husband at Drury College and was in in the same fraternity with him. I almost canceled the appointment, thinking I was overreacting, but I went anyway and had a bunch of blood work done along with a thorough check up. Honestly, deep down inside I knew something was not quite right. I just did not want to admit that or even go there. After the initial visit and blood tests, the doctor's office called and said that there was another test he wanted to do—a twenty-four hour urine test. Hmm. I did not quite get it at that point, but I did not like the direction it was going. It just did not feel right.

I did not keep up with my journaling like I wanted to, but I do want to share with you some of my entries. I am not sure how long after my first unofficial diagnosis that I started journaling, but I am thinking about two months. I think it took that long for it to truly sink in, and for me to collect my emotions.

July 18, 2003

I have wanted to start this since the first time I heard the words, "multiple myeloma." It was a Friday when my doctor called to say he wanted me to see a hematologist. I knew that when a doctor calls, it is significant news. At first he was vague. "You have a certain protein in your blood and the same in your urine, even though in small amounts." "What are you thinking it is?" I asked. Then I heard the dreaded words, "multiple myeloma." He asked if I remembered hearing it or had questions. My mind went back to nursing school and I vaguely remembered. "I know it's not good."

When the phone rang that night and the doctor was on the other end, I knew it could not be a good sign to begin with. Remember Sweet Brown, that lady in the You Tube video who said, "Ain't nobody got time for that?"[14] I knew that my life was about to radically change, whether I had time for it or not. I remember my doctor calmly saying he wanted me to see a specialist. I asked, "What kind?" He said "A hematologist." I knew that was a nice way of saying a "cancer doctor." But I played the game with him. "Why?" I asked, although I knew the answer. He said, "I just want to have her go over the tests and see what she thinks." I remember saying, "Listen, I am a nurse. I can take it. I want to know what you are thinking." He asked if I remembered studying multiple myeloma in nursing school, and I said, "Vaguely, but I know it's not good." Unfortunately, he agreed with me. Needless to say, I was devastated and was practically planning my funeral. I hung up the phone and felt like I was having an out of body experience. It could not be me. It just had to be someone else. I had children. I was practically a Christian my whole life. I never even tried smoking. I did not drink (not even socially). I did not cuss (not even when I hit my funny bone). I did not even go to PG movies. For goodness sakes I was a pastor's wife. Didn't that count for anything? And what about my daughter? I just adopted her from China seven years before. I did not want her to lose her mother again. Then I did what most inquiring minds do and got on my computer. It just about took all my hope away.

July 18, 2003

So I went on the internet. Not a good move. Fear gripped my heart from my head to my toes. I felt paralyzed. Three year survival! I cried. I felt the fear literally choking me. I didn't want to tell anyone, I didn't want to verbally confess it, but I knew I had to tell Chuck.

What really upset me was that I did not even fit the criteria. I was too young (happens in the later decades of life), too white (more prevalent in African-Americans), too female (happens more in men), and too unfair. Therefore, I fell apart. I do not know how long I had a pity party, but I could not eat, cook, sleep, or function for some time.

July 18, 2003

From that moment on everything changed. I lost my appetite, I couldn't sleep, and all I wanted to do was ask God, "Why?" Or say, "This is not happening to me." Then all the good reasons began pouring out. "I have kids. The church needs me. Aimee can't be an orphan again. This is not fair. I've lived a Christian life all my life. I never backslid. I have always helped people. I gave my life to the ministry, etc., etc." I know God was saying, "I've heard all those before."

I had two sons in college. Kyle was attending Evangel University in Springfield, Missouri, and Ryan was at Wheaton College in Wheaton, Illinois. Tyler was in high school, and Aimee was in elementary school. How could I tell them? What would I tell them? Once again, I wish I had kept a journal better. If I would do anything over again, it is that. I started a few times and then stopped. Now I wish I had all the details, all the emotions I was feeling and everything that happened over the years since I started scaling this mountain.

Between chemo brain and menopause brain, there is not much left.

First I had to tell my husband.

July 18, 2003

I didn't want to tell anyone. I didn't want to verbally confess it, but I knew I had to tell Chuck. I don't think it sank in to him like it did to me the first time around. Good old positive Chuck. "Well we will wait and see what the other doctor says. You don't know you have it." First it made me mad. Of course I have it. Why would my doctor even say it? He wouldn't scare me to death if I didn't have it?

My husband did not want me to tell anyone at this point, not even my close friends or family. I reluctantly consented, but then a phone call changed everything. Why are women so emotional? Why is it so easy to let it all spill out so quickly?

July 18, 2003

Chuck did not want anyone to know. I didn't agree. "It's my body," I thought. But he said, "No." So I said, "OK. I won't say anything." Boy this was a first in submission. But a friend of mine called right after the doctor called and she asked how I was feeling. She knew I was going for tests. It just all came out. She was a Spirit-filled, prayer warrior. I needed people praying. Chuck heard the conversation and was upset.

I guess we all handle things differently, and looking back, my husband was having a hard time digesting it all. Sometimes he still does. Don't get me wrong. I still have my days when I just can't figure it out. But as far as blaming God, I just didn't go there.

July 18, 2003

I never got too angry with God, just not understanding Him. But if we could figure Him out, we wouldn't need Him. I know God didn't do this to me, but I knew He had the power to stop it! So why wouldn't He? I cried for a few days. Got up early in the morning. I am not an early riser but I am now. Couldn't think, eat, or clean my house.

Since I already spilled my guts to my friend, Chuck decided we needed to tell our family. Now it was my turn to disagree and start having doubts.

July 18, 2003

So he said, "If you told her we better tell our family." But I wasn't ready for that. 'What if it's not true? Why do this to them?"

The roller coaster of emotions had officially begun. We eventually told each of our children at different times, in different ways, trying to be sensitive to each of their personalities.

July 18, 2003

Ryan came home while I was crying, so I told him. He just hugged me and said, "I'm sorry."

Soon after that we told Kyle and Tyler. Chuck told Kyle while he was in Springfield.

I think my husband made a special trip to Springfield since Kyle was still in school.

July 18, 2003

... and we told Tyler one night while he was at the computer. I told him I had something very serious going on in my body. I laugh now, but he was the only child who asked a question. He said, "Is it ovarian?" To him that was the worst thing that could happen to a woman.

Most vividly, I remember talking with my youngest son Tyler, who was sixteen at the time. I chuckle now at his question, because he is now in medical school. And he still asks the most questions, and wants the most detailed answers.

The hardest person for me to tell was my eighty-three-year-old mother. She was living in Pennsylvania, and I in Missouri. I could not make the trip out there to tell her face to face, like I wanted, so I had to tell her over the phone. Remember, I was her baby. I was supposed to help take care of her since I was the youngest, the healthiest, and the strongest. But she was such a trouper. My mom was such a strong woman, and instead of me trying to console her, she encouraged me and said God was in control, and we would pray for my healing. She also encouraged me not to get discouraged or give up. She believed in a miracle-working God. She was such an encouragement to me, and she always prayed for that miracle up until the day she died at age ninety-three.

As I said, I was an emotional wreck, which was really hard on my family because I was usually very strong emotionally. I did not fall apart every time something bad happened in the family or to me. My kids were not used to seeing me like this. My eldest son seemed to be taking it the best, but he was good at hiding his emotions like most men, and just like his father.

July 18, 2003

Everyone was almost too nice. I got extra hugs from my older sons. Kyle would tease me about exercising more or about his grandchildren and how I was going to baby sit.

My middle son, Ryan, bless his heart, wanted to quit school and take care of me. He was a freshman at Wheaton College. He was the one, years later, who was able to take off work to be with me for two weeks during my stem cell transplant. In fact, all my kids were great! It really brought us together, but it was really difficult and depressing to see my sons being affected emotionally.

July 18, 2003

We chose not to tell Aimee anything at this point, except she knew I was going to the doctor because I was tired.

The only good thing was Aimee was not old enough to grasp it all. And we were very guarded in what we told her. I hated putting any of them through all this. But unfortunately that is just how life is sometimes.

I know they call cancer the big C. But I read something once that said cancer is not the big C. It is really the little c because Christ is "The Big C." And that He is. No matter what your problem, whether physical, spiritual, or emotional, Jesus will bring you through it. I had to pick a life verse for a bio I needed once. It is hard picking one verse but this set of verses has become so dear to my heart, and I hope they bless you. II Corinthians 4:16-18 says, "Therefore we do not lose heart. Though outwardly we are wasting away, yet inwardly we are being renewed day by day. For our light and momentary troubles are achieving for us an eternal glory that far outweighs them all. So we fix our eyes not on what is seen, but on what is unseen, since what is seen is temporary, but what is unseen is eternal." And I like the next verse too. II Corinthians 5:1 says, "For we know that if the earthly tent we live in is destroyed, we have a building from God, an eternal house in heaven, not built by human hands." It really is a win-win situation for the child of God. If we live and enjoy life, that is wonderful, but if we die and go to heaven, then that is so much better. Well, according to Paul it is. Philippians 1:23-24 says, "I am torn between the two: I desire to depart and be with Christ, which is better by far; but it is more necessary for you that I remain in the body." Heaven must not be such a bad place to go. It just gets so comfortable down here. God does want us to enjoy life, and we should. After all, He created it for us, but He also does not want us to fear stepping into eternity when the time comes for us to leave. My mom would always tell me, "I have no doubts about heaven and I am not afraid to die. It is just the getting there part." And when she died God took her so gently, without a struggle. And I thank Him for that. So whatever you think your big letter is, remember God is so much bigger.

CHAPTER 6

How Do You Eat An Elephant?

"The journey of a thousand miles begins with one step."[15]

~ Lao Tzu ~

"One may walk over the highest mountain one step at a time."[16]

~ John Wanamaker ~

Remember the old saying, "How do you eat an elephant?" The answer is, "One bite at a time." Climbing your mountain is like eating an elephant. At first glance it is a very discouraging and impossible-looking situation. Whatever your mountain is, you can do it, one step at a time, because you really do not have much of a choice. You either go forward or jump in a pit and hope no one ever comes to help you out. Whatever your mountain is, it can be conquered. It will not be easy, in any way, shape, or form, but it is possible.

Sometimes your mountain is being built over days, weeks, or years, and other times it is something you literally wake up to. Whether it is the death of a loved one in a tragic accident or finding out you have cancer after weeks and months of not feeling well, the feeling is the same. "I can't do this." Or here is another declaration, "I don't want to do this." Have you ever said that? I have and still do at times. After I was diagnosed with cancer, I was stunned. Paralyzed is a better word. I could not take one step forward, much less try to climb my mountain.

Those verses in II Corinthians 4:8-9 helped me to get up and fight. It says, "We are hard pressed on every side, but not crushed; perplexed, but not in despair; persecuted, but not abandoned; struck down, but not destroyed." It is okay to get knocked down. Well, not really, but it will happen. Just do not stay down for the count. Get up and fight like a man or woman. You may just have had the wind knocked out of you, but take a deep breath and get up. Look around you and see what you have to live for. For me it was my kids. Sorry, honey. I could not imagine my children without a mother. I did not want them to experience that, especially my little girl. How could He allow her to lose a mother a second time? You grasp at anything and everything when your life passes before you, like if you could come up with a good enough reason God would listen to you and do whatever you say.

All I knew was that I had to put this "elephant" into perspective. If I just looked at my prognosis and a few years down the road, it looked like my life was over. Like putting your hands on the shoulders of an hysterical woman and shaking her, or throwing a cold glass of water on a screaming, out-of-control child, I had to do that with my emotions. I had to put my money where my faith was and decide from that moment on I was going to trust God. This was not one of the easier things I have done. I remember the first two weeks I did nothing but cry, sleep, try to eat, and repeat the cycle. Then one day I got up and verbally cried out to God and said, "God, please heal me. And if you cannot heal me physically, then heal me emotionally." It was almost instantaneous. The fear left immediately and I knew in my heart that God was going to help me through it. It was a miracle. Not quite the one I wanted, but a miracle none the less. I wish I didn't give Him a choice!

The devil tried to destroy me with fear. He still tries. There is an experience I had that I have not shared with many people. Part of the reason is because in the past, if someone would have shared a similar incident with me, I would have said it was due to the pepperoni pizza they ate before they went to bed. I was always skeptical of "weird spiritual encounters" that people say they had. But since it happened to me, I am a believer. It was within the first few weeks of my diagnosis, so I was still a bit weepy and slept a bit more than usual. I was not taking any kind of medication, just in case you were wondering. It happened early in the morning, right after my husband left for work. I was still in bed and was in a semi-conscious state. I was either, half asleep and trying to wake up, or half-awake and trying to go to sleep. Suddenly I heard the most hideous sounds I have ever heard. There was screeching and screaming in high-pitched demonic voices. There were many of them. I have never heard anything like that before. I knew they were coming from the pit of hell. Chills went up and down my spine. Fear gripped my whole being. My bedroom looked hazy. I tried to wake myself up but I could not. Instead, I felt a force pulling me towards the edge of the bed, but I kept trying to break free. I tried to scream, but nothing came out. It was as if I was completely paralyzed from my head to my toes. But there was one thing I could still do, so I did it. I started earnestly praying in my mind and finally was able to yell, "NO!" I immediately woke up in a cold sweat, still shaking from the experience, but I knew then that God was greater than any demonic force that would try to destroy me. It was an experience I will never forget and one that I do not want to repeat.

I know there may be some of you who are a bit skeptical. I was one of those people not too long ago. Just as much as heaven is for real, so are the demonic forces that are invading our world. Ephesians 6:11-12 is a command to all of us. It says, "Put on the full armor of God, so that you can take your stand against the devil's schemes. For our struggle is not against flesh and blood, but against the rulers, against the authorities, against the powers of this dark world and against the spiritual forces of evil in the heavenly realms." Why would Paul charge us to do this? He did it because of the seriousness of the situation.

It wasn't a suggestion. It was a command. If we think the devil is just a man in a red suit with a pitch fork, we will be unaware of his schemes and traps he has set for us. His job description is to do all he can to take as many souls with him to hell. His other job description is to discourage believers and make us think God does not answer prayer, or even care. We do not have to fear the enemy's power because God's power is so much greater. We just need to stand our ground and be prepared to fight. Most of all, we need to know Jesus defeated him when He gave his life as the final sacrifice for our sins.

We just never know the struggles that people experience. That is why it is so important that we support each other when we are going through our trials. I received so much encouragement from my family and friends. I still do. I received so many cards, letters, text messages, and phone calls that have carried me through to this very moment. And they still keep coming. Sometimes you do not know what to say or do when someone is going through a difficult trial, so you tend to do nothing. But take it from someone who has been on both ends. A short phone call, an encouraging text, a card, a letter, offering to take them to a doctor's appointment, cleaning their house, or even making a simple meal, are some things that can make each day a little more bearable for that person who is struggling to survive.

August 11, 2003

Ryan came in and said, "Boy, you are popular." He just brought the mail in. I asked him, "How many prayers would it take for God to heal me?" He looked at me and without hesitation said, "One." I said, "What do you mean?" He said, "God heard you the first time you prayed. It only takes one prayer, Mom, the first one."

It is so true. God hears us the first time we call out to Him. He is not-hard-of hearing. He does not need hearing aids. We may sometimes think He has selective hearing, like our kids and husbands do at times, but He does not. And God does not forget, except all the bad things which are forgiven. He has the best memory in the universe. And that is what makes it so hard to figure Him out sometimes.

If you do not think you have anything or anyone to live for, then look at it this way. Do not let the devil win. John 10:10 says "The thief comes only to steal and kill and destroy; I have come that they may have life, and have it to the full." The devil wants to take you out either physically, spiritually, or emotionally, but God wants you to enjoy life to the fullest. It does not matter what your situation is or how many breaths you have left. You still have a lot of living to do, so keep climbing!

CHAPTER 7

THINGS AREN'T ALWAYS THE WAY THEY APPEAR

"When one door closes, another opens. But we often look so regretfully upon the closed door that we don't see the one which has opened for us."[17]

~ Alexander Graham Bell ~

I love the story in the Old Testament of Elisha and his servant. It is found in II Kings 6:15-18. I do not usually use the King James Version. Sorry for you die-hard King James people, but I love it for this reference.

"And when the servant of the man of God was risen early, and gone forth, behold, a host with horses and chariots was round about the city. And his servant said unto him, 'Alas, my master! How shall we do?' And he answered, 'Fear not; for they that are with us are more than they that are with them.' And Elisha prayed, and said, 'Jehovah, I pray Thee, open his eyes, that he may see.' And Jehovah opened the eyes of the young man; and he saw: and, behold, the mountain was full of horses and chariots of fire round about Elisha."

This true story reminds me of a book I read several years ago, *This Present Darkness,* by Frank Peretti. It really painted a wonderful word picture and opened your spiritual eyes to what is actually happening all around us every day, especially the spiritual battles that are going on for us. So many times we only see with our carnal eyes. And things are not always the way they seem. Take, for instance, when I would try to wake up my daughter Aimee in the morning for school. I would say, "Aimee, it is time to get up!" She would move or grunt, so I knew she heard me. A few minutes later I would hear the shower running, so I assumed she was up. A few minutes turned into a lot of minutes, so I thought she was taking a really long shower, until one day I went into her room to check on her. To my surprise and annoyance, the shower was running with her still sleeping in her bed! I soon realized that this was not the first time she did it. What I thought was happening was not reality. Something else was happening. Really, nothing was happening! She just wanted me to think it was.

Even when we think nothing is happening, God is always working. We need to open up our spiritual eyes or put on our spiritual contact lenses. How is God working? What is God really doing? How is my situation bringing glory to His name? How is God using me to be an example? How can I change the way I look at my situation?

It never ceases to amaze me how God works. Take my situation. I have an incurable cancer. My church has been praying for me for eleven years. I have had prayer teams headed by a wonderful woman of God in my church. There would be different teams that would come to my home every day for one hour to lay hands on me and pray for me. They did this for six weeks. It was an amazing time of prayer and petition to heaven. One day I was feeling terrible, for them and for me. They have been praying for over a decade, along with people in my community, without seeing God heal me. I was worried that it would affect them negatively and that it might affect my witness. Maybe they would give up or feel God could not do it. But instead, people tell me that I am an inspiration to them. They have been watching me. Some with magnifying glasses, I am sure. I have not discouraged them. I have, unbeknownst to me, encouraged them, because they see my positive attitude and endurance. Imagine that. Good thing they do not see me all the time. What the devil meant for bad, God is turning out for good. The devil tries to play mind games with you, but do not believe him. I have a win-win situation, and so do you. If I live I will continue to be a testimony and inspiration. And if I die, I go to heaven, but I will leave a legacy and pray souls would be saved by it.

I love the lyrics to Nichole
Nordeman's song, "Legacy."

"I want to leave a legacy,
How will they remember me?
Did I choose to love?
Did I point to you enough to
make a mark on things?"[18]

I get choked up every time I hear that song. I am crying now. We are leaving a legacy, whether we realize it or not. We are an example with every breath that we take, whether we are a good one or not. Unlike Paul, I would rather continue to be a testimony here on this earth. But you really cannot lose, and the devil cannot win. You can get discouraged, but do not ever think God is not working. He never slumbers or sleeps. What do you think He does on His down time? He does not have any. He does not get tired. Do not think for a minute that He is not working. It just may not be like you want it. It's not always like I want it.

We are all here for a purpose, although at times I wonder if I am really making a difference in people's lives. But then God comes through again gently reminding me I still have work to do. Sometimes I minister to people and then they literally disappear and I wonder, "Did they make it? What are they doing with their life now? Are they even alive? Did I even make a difference?"

One morning I was at a local restaurant with my husband. We were at the register waiting to check out when the cashier looked at me and asked if I remembered her. At that moment I did not. I wish I could remember her exact words to me that changed my life in less than five minutes. She began by saying that I was such a big influence on her life nine years ago.

Where was I with this lady nine years ago? And then she told me the circumstances and the light bulb switched on. At that moment I remembered. Tears began to flow down my cheeks and I couldn't stop them. Soon she had to take off her glasses because tears were blurring her vision and she was trying her best to be professional at the register. I never had such an emotional experience checking out of a restaurant before. From the corner of my eyes I could see all across the dining room people were watching this unusual check out scene. She told me that she had held on to what I had told her. I had no idea what I told her nine years ago. She said I encouraged her to believe God to restore her family and her life. And she did. She held on to that promise all these years and God was faithful. Now she has a good job and is doing well. She said, "You are an amazing woman and I don't know where I would be if our paths did not cross." She thanked me again, and as I walked out of the restaurant I couldn't stop crying. She also said she was praying for me because she heard I was sick. Wow. I needed that encouragement especially on that day.

We are leaving a legacy. We are here for a reason. We never know how our words can greatly influence another person's life. Sometimes we may never see the fruit of our labor. I am so glad our paths crossed again. God is faithful and she will never know that she was as much an encouragement to me as I was to her. Now I have another prayer warrior. Never doubt how God can use you. Never doubt how He works. Never doubt Him. If you ever do remember John.

What about my situation, you ask? How can God be working? It's not fair! Glad you asked those questions. Remember you have something in common with John the Baptist. He was waiting to get his head cut off because he preached the truth about Jesus. Wouldn't you say that is definitely not fair? He knew his situation demanded a miracle from the only One who could do that for him. But then he began to wonder if Jesus was who He really said He was. He did not say, "Jesus, I know you are God and have miraculous power, so I would like you to show some of that potential now for me, your cuz." No, he was wavering in his faith. He was scared of his predicament, so he asked, "Are You who You really say You are?" Remember, John was a great man of God, but he also was very human, just flesh and blood like you and me.

I hate to pick on him so much, but I want you to see it is acceptable to be human and have those negative feelings. And if John, one of the greatest men who ever lived, could doubt, so can we. This guy did summersaults in utero when Mary, Jesus' mother, visited Elizabeth, John's mother, when they were both expecting. Luke 1:41 says, "When Elizabeth heard Mary's greeting, the baby leaped in her womb, and Elizabeth was filled with the Holy Spirit." Amazing! I am sure Elizabeth told John that story over and over again as he was growing up. He probably would say, "Mommy tell me that story again about what happened when I was living inside your tummy."

My mom would tell me the same stories over and over again. Her favorites were when I almost fell off the cliff and about her having a miscarriage before I was born. I think she always was reinforcing in me that I was here for a reason. I am sure your mom has told you a few stories, and you are keeping the tradition with your children too.

After all that happened in his life, John the great preacher still had a moment of doubt. It might have been for a split second, maybe longer. When his situation was desperate he wanted to make sure about Jesus. What about us? We see God work. He does miracles today. The greatest miracle is a person being born again. He has answered prayer in each of our lives. But when tragedy touches us that is a ten on a scale of one to ten, then everything changes. It sometimes alters our whole perspective, and from time to time causes us to doubt. You may be saying, “It is just too big! Is Jesus who He really says He is? Does He really have the power to help me? And if He does, then why isn’t He doing something, now?”

Remember again what Jesus told John? In my own words He was saying, “Sorry cousin, but more blessed are those who do not see, yet believe. John, in a few minutes this trial will pass and you will get your reward. Just keep the faith and simply remember everything you have seen Me do." So I say to each one of you, remember what God has done for you in the past, trust Him for the present, and never stop believing Him for the future. That is so hard sometimes. In fact it is hard all the time. And if you have never doubted, you probably will at some point in your life. And if you are questioning God now, all I can say is hold on tight and keep the faith. God is working.

I like that song by Don Moen,
"God Will Make A Way."

"God will make a way when
there seems to be no way.
He works in ways we cannot see,
He will make a way for me.
He will be my guide.
Hold me closely to His side.
With love and strength for each new day,
He will make a way, He will make a way."[19]

What a great guide to have while climbing our mountain. The catch is God does things the way He wants to and not always the way we want it to happen.

Let me just get this out of the way and say, "God did not create evil or sickness." I know you know that, but if you want to blame someone, blame the devil, or Adam and Eve, or yourself, in some situations. Now hold on and listen to this. James 1:13-15 says, "When tempted, no one should say, 'God is tempting me.' For God cannot be tempted by evil, nor does he tempt anyone; but each person is tempted when they are dragged away by their own evil desire and enticed. Then, after desire has conceived, it gives birth to sin; and sin, when it is full-grown, gives birth to death." Sometimes we blame God, the devil, or anyone else we can blame, for things that we cause ourselves. Ouch! Then we get mad at Him if He does not help us. Sort of like the alcoholic who gets cirrhosis of the liver and then gets mad at God. Or what about the smoker who develops lung cancer? Or the teenager who contracts an STD because of sexual promiscuity? The list can go on and on. Now if you are in one of these situations, God will not leave you. He still can heal you, or help you through this, just do not get mad at Him for causing it. I know where sin and sickness come from. Can God stop it? Absolutely! It is the allowing part I cannot understand. I often think I have some pretty good ideas to help God fix things. Don't you? I like that jingle Ford used to have. It said, "Ford has a better idea." But for now you just have to believe that God has the best idea, so you can stop trying to figure things out on your own and trust God's heart, and keep climbing up.

CHAPTER 8

Those Clouds Are Not Really There!

"The pessimist complains about the wind; the optimist expects it to change; the realist adjusts the sails."[20]

~ William Arthur Ward ~

"It is what it is."

~ Not sure who said it but I use it a lot. ~

I have had many people tell me many things since I have had cancer this past decade. Most of it has been good, but there are a few things that have not been, let us just say, beneficial or encouraging to my emotional status. We must be very careful what we say to people who are going through catastrophic situations, some that may even take their life, or the life of their loved one. I know most people do mean well. I like the revised statement of sticks and stones. It says, "Sticks and stones may break your bones, but words can hurt you in a different way."[21] I do not want to offend any of you, but I am just sharing out of my heart what I have learned. I hope it all lines up with scripture, although I do not think it will line up with some of your theology. For that I apologize. You can write a sequel to this book and then I will be offended.

While writing this book, I have been visiting my kids in St. Lucia for two weeks. In fact, you will hear me talk about St. Lucia several times throughout this book. I wrote a big part of it while I was there. It must have been the sunshine and scenery. For the past few days it has been raining on an off and probably will be in the next few minutes, but I decided to take a chance and take a walk around the apartment complex anyway. When I got to the end of the road where I was going to turn and go back home, I spotted Sofia, the secretary of the facility my kids are renting from. She is a wonderful woman of God and a great prayer warrior. I shouted, "Good morning!" She waved and said, "How are you this morning Mrs. Whitmire? It looks like it is going to rain!" I smiled and said I was trying to get a short walk in before it did. Now when she said that, I could have said, "No it doesn't. The sun is shining." She would have made a quick call to my son to tell him that there was something wrong with his mother. She knew the weather pattern in St. Lucia. You do not have to be a meteorologist to know that when the clouds are black, you hear thunder in the heavens, and feel the wind pick up, that it is probably going to rain, since it does that quite often. For you optimists, including my husband, this will make you cringe. Even Jesus said you would know when it was going to rain. Luke

12:54 says, "He said to the crowd, 'When you see a cloud rising in the west immediately you say, 'It's going to rain.' And it does." That was the beginning of meteorology.

I think you know where I am going with this. I believe we need to have faith. Hebrews 11:6 says, "And without faith it is impossible to please God, because anyone who comes to him must believe that He exists and that He rewards those who earnestly seek him." But how much faith? That is the million dollar question. Here is what Jesus said in Luke 17:6, "He replied, 'If you have faith as small as a mustard seed, you can say to this mulberry tree, 'Be uprooted and planted in the sea,' and it will obey you." Do you know how small a mustard seed is? Very tiny. Jesus said it was the smallest of seeds. This statement interested me, because in my study I found out that the orchid seed is smaller than the mustard seed, so why did He say that? Depending on your translation you might have the word "smaller" as in the New International Version and several other translations, or the word "least" as quoted in the King James Version.

But the Greek word is the same. It is "mikros," which means small or little.[22] And that is the point. A mustard seed is a very small seed.

Jesus was not comparing the mustard seed to every seed in the known world. He was comparing them to seeds that a local, Palestinian farmer might have sowed in his field. The black mustard seed was the smallest seed ever sown by a first-century farmer in that part of the world during that time. Luke 13:18-19 says, "Then Jesus asked, 'What is the kingdom of God like? What shall I compare it to?' It is like a mustard seed, which a man took and planted in his garden. It grew and became a tree, and the birds perched in its branches." The black mustard seed in Israel could grow up to twelve feet tall. That would be large enough to hold a bird's nest in it. Jesus tried to use everyday language to convey simple truths. Just like we talk about a beautiful "sunset" when scientifically, we know that the sun never actually "sets." In Matthew 13 Jesus was talking to everyday people, not to an international conference of botanists.[23] I share this with you just in case you ever questioned this word. My conclusion: I think the point Jesus was trying to make is that the mustard seed is a tiny seed, and I know you have that much faith, and so do I.

Jesus also healed people when there was unbelief or no faith. Mark 9:24 says, "Immediately the boy's father exclaimed, 'I do believe; help me overcome my unbelief.'" Did you ever feel like that? I have, and that is when my friends have to be my Aaron and Hur. I love that story in Exodus 17:12 that says, "When Moses' hands grew tired, they took a stone and put it under him and he sat on it. Aaron and Hur held his hands up—one on one side, one on the other—so that his hands remained steady till sunset." Not that I am saying I am Moses, but you get the picture. You can read the whole story to get the unabridged version, but, in a nutshell, the Israelites were having a battle. Moses noticed that when he held his hands up the good guys kept winning, but when he let them down the bad guys started winning. The only problem was Moses was human and his arms were getting tired. Have you ever tried to hold up your arms for several hours? So Aaron and Hur held up his arms, one on each side. What a great picture of Christian friendship. I have quite a few Aarons and Hurs. When I am having a bad day I tell them, "You need to be my Aaron or Hur today." I have been in my battle for eleven years. There is no way I could hold up my hands that long without any help, and neither can you.

Jesus healed in so many ways, so there is no real pattern that we can patent to say this is how it will always be done. I think He did that for a reason. With Hezekiah they called for the physicians to do a medical treatment. And a prophet told him to do it. Not just any prophet, but the prophet Isaiah. II Kings 20:7 says, "Then Isaiah said, 'Prepare a poultice of figs.' They did so and applied it to the boil, and he recovered." Why did He use figs? God definitely could have healed him without it, but that is not how He did it this time. And He can use any medical treatment or other human measures to do it. Now I want to say, like Paul says, this is my opinion. In 1 Cor. 7:12, Paul says, "To the rest I say this (I, not the Lord). . ." or in 1 Cor. 7:25 he says ". . . I have no command of the Lord, but I give an opinion as one who by the mercy of the Lord is trustworthy." This is what I have learned through my tenure with my trial: People may look at you and say, "You do not have enough faith." "You do not have cancer." "Don't claim it." These are some of the statements that do not really help the sick person in any way, shape, or form. Besides all that, it really is not true.

Jesus asked blind Bartimaeus a weird question in Mark 10:51. "What do you want me to do for you?" Jesus asked him. The blind man said, "Rabbi, I want to see." Did Jesus not notice he was blind? Why would He even ask him that question? Jesus knew he was blind, but He wanted him to confess with his mouth what he needed. Jesus wanted him to admit he was blind even though it was pretty obvious. He wanted him to say what he wanted, even though He knew what he needed. And after that, He healed him. I don't know why he asked Bartimaeus that question but healed others without asking. Or why did

Naaman have to dip seven times in the Jordan River, which was dirtier than other rivers? Did it have magical powers? I do not think so. And he got mad and had a terrible attitude toward God's prophet, but God still came through and healed him. On the other hand, I do believe that lack of faith and harboring bitterness in your heart are definite hindrances to having your prayers answered. Any prayer. We should definitely confess our sins, make things right with others, pray earnestly for God to remove our trial, heal our sickness or whatever we need, BUT IF NOT. . .

I love the story of the three Hebrew young men. They had such faith in God that even if they thought He was not going to deliver them, they still were not going to bow. Daniel 3:16-18 says, "Shadrach, Meshach and Abednego replied to him, 'King Nebuchadnezzar, we do not need to defend ourselves before you in this matter. If we are thrown into the blazing furnace, the God we serve is able to deliver us from it, and He will deliver us from Your Majesty's hand. But even if He does not, we want you to know, Your Majesty, that we will not serve your gods or worship the image of gold you have set up.'" Wow! So what if I say, "Even if God does not heal me, I still will serve him!" Is that lack of faith? I do not think so.

I do believe God can heal but people die from illnesses every day. My mom always said, "If God healed everyone, no one would die." Billy Graham will die with Parkinson's disease one day, unless God heals him. Does that mean he has a lack of faith? I do not think so. Jesus did not heal his earthly father, either. There is no mention of him in Jesus' later years. Jesus asked John to take care of his mother at the foot of the cross. Joseph must have already died. That was Jesus' father. The bottom line is we just cannot figure God out all the time or try to put Him in a box. We love and serve God because He is God, not for what He can or will do for us. There is a song written by Shirley Caesar called, "It's Been Worth Just Having The Lord In My Life." I have been blessed by this song since I was a teenager. It really makes you think about your commitment to serving the Lord.

"But if heaven never were promised to me,
Even God's promise to live eternally.
It's been worth just having
the Lord in my life."[24]

If heaven never was promised to you and He told you He was not going to change your situation, would you still have faith and serve Him? I hope you are shouting, "Yes!" Amen?

So what are you going to do until God comes through? That song by John Waller, "While I'm Waiting" says it all. It does not say, "I am waiting for you to heal me, or deliver me, so wake me up when You do." It says, "While I'm waiting I will serve You." Just because you have cancer, or lupus, or your husband left you, or (you can fill it in with your mountain) does not mean you do not continue to serve God. If your trial is hindering you from moving forward, you will miss out on some of the most wonderful blessings of your life.

St. Lucian beaches are beautiful and the island is surrounded by lush tropical plants, but not everything is beautiful here. I have learned so much just from watching the day to day life of the people that live here. Unless you are rich and famous, most citizens have a hard life here. This fertile island is about twenty seven miles long and fourteen miles wide. It is almost like a third world county, except for the exotic resorts. You can drive through the island from one end to the other in a few hours. There were more cars than I thought there would be, but a lot of people walk or take a bus.

I was intrigued with their transit system, and I use that term loosely. They do have some designated bus stops, but it seemed liked you could make your own bus stop by standing anywhere on the road where you want to be picked up. Pretty handy. Actually it is more like waving down a taxi in New York City. And their city buses are vans, or sometimes cars. A lot of people hitchhike a ride to get anywhere. But what was really intriguing is they do not all wait on the transportation system to come to them. Most of them probably cannot afford it. Remember, time is relative here. Might as well throw your watches out the window. No one is really in a hurry except if there is a car behind you when you are driving too slow. You see people everywhere walking up the mountain, and it is very steep in places. No bathrooms on the way. Not many convenience stores to get a cold pop. I saw several men carrying machetes, but I was told it was for "clearing brush along the way." Sure. It might take them a good part of their day to go a few miles. They may start walking and if someone picks them up, great, but if not, they will get there themselves, on foot when they get there. My son's housekeeper walks about a mile or so down the mountain every day just to get to the bus stop. And it is hot, uncomfortably hot most of the time. Then she walks up the mountain when she goes home.

Isn't that a lesson for us? We all have trials. We could just sit there and wait and maybe never get anywhere in life, waiting for God to deliver us, or we can serve God while we are waiting. God's deliverance can come in so many ways. Sometimes we think God has to do it the way we want Him to, and we miss out.

I like the illustration of the man waiting on the roof for help. I don't know who wrote it. But here is how it goes. "A fellow was stuck on his rooftop during a flood. He was praying to God for help. Soon a man in a rowboat came by and the fellow shouted to the man on the roof, 'Jump in, I can save you.' The stranded fellow shouted back, 'No, it's OK, I'm praying to God and He is going to save me.' So the rowboat went on. Then a motorboat came by. The fellow in the motorboat shouted, 'Jump in, I can save you.' To this the stranded man said, 'No thanks, I'm praying to God and He is going to save me. I have faith.' So the motorboat went on. Then a helicopter came by and the pilot shouted down, 'Grab this rope and I will lift you to safety.' To this the stranded man again replied, 'No thanks, I'm praying to God and He is going to save me. I have faith.' So the helicopter reluctantly flew away. Soon the water rose above the rooftop and the man drowned. He went to heaven. He finally got his chance to discuss this whole situation with God, at which point he exclaimed, 'I had faith in You but You didn't save me, You let me drown. I don't understand why!' To this God replied, 'I sent you a rowboat and a motorboat and a helicopter. What more did you expect?'" Why do we always put God in a box? God will do things His way, and all we have to do is open our eyes and heart to see it.

My son is in medical school. I keep trying to get him to go into oncology. Do we go to the doctor when we are sick? Hezekiah did. We do, too, for some things. Is that lack of faith? Some would say yes. Luke was a doctor. But there never were any negative references to a doctor in the Bible that I can remember. In fact, this is what Jesus said in Matthew 9:12, "Jesus said, 'It is not the healthy who need a doctor, but the sick.'" He could have said, "The sick do not need a doctor anymore, because I am here." And Jesus healed so many people. But all the disciples died horrible martyr's deaths, except for John. Why? We just do not know the mind of God. So while we are waiting, we continue to press onward, till God delivers us, calls us home, or the rapture happens, which I am hoping for. It could happen soon the way the world is deteriorating and prophetic signs are taking place. Do not stop believing for your miracle, and please be encouraged. Let God give you the strength you need to serve Him while you are waiting. So keep trudging up the mountain, and take someone with you. It makes the going so much easier.

CHAPTER 9

God Is Bigger Than The Boogie Man

"The presence of fear does not mean you have no faith. Fear visits everyone. But make your fear a visitor and not a resident."[25]

~ Max Lucado ~

Jesus had a special style of speaking. He was more of a teacher, although at times He preached with authority. He liked to use word pictures, or parables, to get His point across to help people understand biblical truths. However, at times the crowds still did not get it.

How many of you were afraid of the "Boogie Man" when you were little? I was. There's a great Veggie Tales kid's song that is called, "God Is Bigger Than The Boogie Man." It is a perfect song for kids, and it is a fitting word picture for them to understand what fear is, because most kids are afraid of the dark and that is exactly when the Boogie Man appears, whoever he is. If we can explain to them that God is bigger than the Boogie Man, or their biggest fear, then they do not have to be afraid of anything else that will happen to them, because God will take care of them.

Look at it this way. I was visiting my son and his wife in St. Lucia. I was sitting in their gazebo one morning, waiting for their housekeeper to meet me for a Bible study. It was early, or at least early for me, about 7:20 a.m. I was surrounded by lush greenery, coconut and banana trees, birds and bugs. Oh, lizards too! I am terrified of bugs, especially flying ones, or birds, if they get too close. Don't laugh; just get the word picture here. There was this lone black bird who was sitting at the table next to me. I was on my iPad and he was doing what birds do, whatever that is. That was fine as long as he did not join me at my table. I think I said something to him like, "Hello, little bird." I never thought he could understand me. Then he turned and cocked his head, trying to understand my accent, and perched on the chair closer to me. I tried to shoo him away, but then he hopped right on the middle of the table where I was sitting. We were face to face. This was too weird. I could not believe it. He perched himself on it like he was a new centerpiece for the table. I was stunned. Wish I knew what I said to him to get him there. For a split second I wanted to get up and move away from him. If it was a flying bug I would not have thought twice. But then I thought, this is silly. I am at least fifty times bigger than him, probably more since I gained weight on this vacation. I readjusted my seat on purpose, hoping he would not come any closer. I think he got the picture. He looked at me, cocked his head again, and then flew away. Then I got this word picture.

That little black bird is like the devil. First, he tries to get our attention from a distance. Then he hangs around and tries to act chummy. He slowly tries to get closer and closer. Before long he is right in front of us. Sometimes he tries to be our friend. He does not want us to be afraid of him. There are times we need to run from him, but there are also times when we just need to stand our ground and say, "You can't hurt me or scare me." James 4:7 says it best. "Submit yourselves, then, to God. Resist the devil, and he will flee from you." We know in theory God in us is definitely bigger than any person, place, or thing in our life that may be trying to destroy us either physically, spiritually, or emotionally. I John 4:4 says, "You, dear children, are from God and have overcome them, because the one who is in you is greater than the one who is in the world." You know, the strange thing is that the devil knows who is stronger. The demons know it, too. James 2:19 says, "You believe that there is one God. Good! Even the demons believe that—and shudder." So who needs convincing? We do! We have so much more power than we realize. May God help all of us to see it, believe it, and use it for His glory.

CHAPTER 10

So Glad I Didn't Know That

"Ignorance is bliss."[26]

~ Thomas Gray ~

I was sitting in a St. Lucian Pentecostal Church this morning. The service started at 8 a.m. and ended at 11:30 a.m. No fans, no air conditioner, no breeze, no bulletins, and you are standing most of the time. Would we tolerate that every Sunday? I get restless when my husband hits the thirty minute mark for preaching in a climate controlled church. People usually complain that it is too cold. This is their agenda for the week: First, immediately after service there was an invitation to prayer and fasting till 5 p.m. When the pastor's wife made the announcement, she started out by saying, "We would like to invite each one of you to a . . ." I thought she was going to invite us to a Sunday potluck dinner. Isn't that what Christians do after church? But she was inviting us to a prayer and fasting meeting. Are you kidding me? Having a five hour prayer meeting after a three and a half hour service? Then on Monday there was prayer time, on Tuesday there was, guess what? You are right, prayer time, along with a women's Bible study. And on Wednesday, prayer and Bible study for everyone. Then the men's group and youth group met another night. I believe there was something happening on Thursday or Friday, a teaching seminar on Saturday, and back to church on Sunday. Almost every day in church! Kind of reminds you of the book of Acts, doesn't it?

Don't these people have a life outside the church? Sure do. They work all day and go to church almost every night. In fact one of my son's professors was there, a teacher from the school my daughter-in-law works at, and a lady I met the day before working in a store I went to. It was an awesome service and the pastor's sermon was on healing. My daughter-in-law looked at me and said, "You came at the right time!" God is so good. After a lengthy, but encouraging sermon, we had communion. Of course, being a nurse, I wondered if they did it "Last Supper" style, so I was relieved when I saw they used the individual plastic disposable cups like we do. Of course they used real bread, and I wondered if they washed their hands before they broke it. My mind just does not stop. This was the way they did it. You went up and took your cup and piece of bread, and if you needed healing you stayed up front! I never miss an opportunity to pray for my healing, especially in a praying church. For a split second I thought, "I am really going to stand out in an all-Lucian church." To my surprise, there were about fifty or more people standing in the front for healing and they filled in behind me! My daughter-in-law asked if she could stand with me. That made me cry.

It was an especially emotional time for me, because a few years ago I had a dream that I was in a foreign country. I had been going to missions trips to Mexico, so at first I thought it was a Mexican church, but the people in my dream were darker. In my dream I went up to be prayed for on the right hand side of the church. It was full. I started weeping, because I was in that church in my dream and I found myself standing on the right side of the church for prayer! Although I did not feel any lightning bolts, God was just reconfirming that He was with me. He cares about what I am going through and He will see me through. Every time I get a little discouraged, God does little things like that to encourage me. Please do not lose heart. No matter how long you have been going through your trial, God will come through. It may not always be the way we think it should be. It may not be when we want it to happen. Sometimes He comes through when we least expect it.

I could have stayed home this morning, because I did not sleep well the night before, and then I had to get up early and sit in a hot church for three and a half hours. I do not tolerate the heat very well, but I am so glad I did. I received such a blessing, and I felt like I went to church this morning. God does not allow mountains in your path for you to look at and admire. Neither does He want them to paralyze you. He can move them, but if not, then start climbing.

God also has a great sense of humor. Lately my white blood count (WBC) has been lower than it has been the last few years, because my myeloma is starting to resurface, so I am really careful about germs. When your WBC is low, or you have cancer or any other auto immune disease that compromises your immune system, it can decrease your ability to fight infection as well as a normal healthy person. Remember, I mentioned earlier that they had disposable plastic communion cups. Well, at the end of the service the pastor's wife made an important announcement, "We are missing one communion cup. Please return it to an usher." My daughter-in-law and I exchanged glances and "Oh My Goodness" expressions. My stomach started churning. They actually reused plastic disposable communion cups! And I drank out of one. I thought, "I went up to be healed and now I exposed myself to more germs." That verse in the Bible came to my mind, Mark 16:18, "If you drink any deadly poison it will not harm you." We must learn to trust God in every situation and laugh when He does things His way to help you do just that.

CHAPTER 11

Fly Delta And Keep Climbing

"You've got to expect things are going to go wrong. And we always need to prepare ourselves for handling the unexpected."[27]

~ Neil Armstrong ~

I was buckling myself into my seat to fly home when a pre- flight video came on. The airline I flew home on was Delta. I am not advertising for them, but a phrase caught my eye. On the screen the Delta logo came on, but it was the words that followed that caught my attention. It said, "Fly Delta and keep climbing!" How appropriate for this book. No matter what, keep climbing. There will be many difficulties in life and situations that will try to slow you down, but just set your pace and keep climbing! I have been climbing my mountain for many years. Some years the climb has been fairly smooth, but other years have been very difficult. Sometimes my life is more like a roller coaster. Just when you catch your breath one minute, you are ready to lose it again on the next loop. Or like this flight. It has been a pretty smooth flight, but the pilot just came on to tell us to get back to our seats and fasten our seat belts because we were headed for some turbulence, and the ride would be a bit bumpy. Of course Jesus, our Pilot, said that in John 16:3, "In this world you *will* have trouble." We just do not know when. None of us know what a day may bring. It would be nice if God would say, "Hey, there is something that is going to make you fall on your knees in a few days, so get ready!" Unfortunately, it does not happen like that. One day you may think everything is fine with your kids; the next day you find out your child is on drugs. One day you feel like you are on the mountain top enjoying the view, the next day you fall into an unforeseen pit. One day you see a friend at a restaurant, the next day you hear of his fatal automobile accident. Or like a good friend of mine, one day she was having a great time on vacation with her husband and kids, the next minute she was in the emergency room and a young widow was born. For me, one day I thought I was just tired, the next thing I hear the doctor say is, "You have an incurable cancer."

Everything seemed to be going fine after my stem cell transplant three years ago. I will talk more about that later. For a year and a half I enjoyed being medicine free and I felt really good. Almost normal. A transplant can last anywhere from two months to sometimes ten or more years for some people. I was praying for the latter. After about a year and a half my blood work gradually started showing signs that the transplant was losing its effectiveness and the disease was becoming active again. Every month my counts were gradually moving away from the normal range into the worrisome range. Actually, the disease was quietly hiding and never left. The counts that should have been staying up were going down and the ones that should be going down were starting to climb. I was more annoyed, mad, and frustrated at this "Series of Unfortunate Events," although, at times, fear would try to convince me my life was over, again. Doesn't God know I have things to do for Him? Honestly, I do not know what God is doing or thinking, but I know He is good and He is faithful. Here is a poem God gave me to help remind me to keep fighting and keep climbing.

Finish

You started this race
With an easy tread.
And trusted in God.
You believed what He said.

At first it was easy
You felt so secure.
But soon doubts and trials
Made your pathway obscure.

The way became narrow
The road became steep.
Now you're tempted to quit
As you fall down and weep.

But God never promised
A smooth easy road.
He just promised to guide you
And carry your load.

Rest if you must
And slow down a bit,
But never lay down
And be tempted to quit.

For there's a prize to be won.
There are more miles to make.
Finish what you started.
Whatever it takes.

And no matter what trials
May happen to you,
Fix your eyes on the Savior
And He'll carry you through.

So when the road ahead gets steep or rocky, you can slow down, but never, ever quit.

CHAPTER 12

I Love Shadows

"When walking through the 'valley of shadows,' remember, a shadow is cast by a Light."[28]

~ H.K. Barclay ~

I remember as a child, when it was way past my bedtime, my mom would say, "It's time to turn off the lights and go to sleep?" But I just was not ready yet. I would sneak a flashlight and make shadow animals on the wall to help me fall asleep. Did you ever do that? Really, I was just buying more time to stay awake. I love that verse in Psalms 23:4 now more than ever, because it says, "Even though I walk through the valley of the *shadow* of death, I fear no evil, for You are with me. . ." I never appreciated shadows that much before, and I never really grasped the meaning of this verse until I was going through my valley. It is so funny, not ha, ha, funny, but have you ever read a verse for the first time, even though it was not really the first time you read it? Did you ever think, "Why didn't I see that before?" You might have read the same verse a dozen times before, but this time a new meaning jumps off the page! That's what I love about the Bible.

What is so important about a shadow in this verse? "Shadows are formed when an opaque object is placed in the path of light rays. The rays go past the edges of the object and make an outline which forms a shadow."[29] Did you know there are two types of shadows? I did not. "A positive shadow, which is what you see following you on a sunny day, and a negative shadow, which is what you see when the moon eclipses the sun and leaves a lighted circle surrounded by a shadow. Positive shadows are outlined by the light that is able to pass around the object, leaving a darker area where the light is unable to reach in the center."[30] Are you seeing the significance of a shadow yet?

First of all, David says he is walking *through* The Valley of The Shadow of Death. David was not dying in this psalm, but he sure thought he could be. In fact there were many times David thought he was going to die. Every time those thoughts would come into his head, I think he held on to the promises of God that he was going to be God's chosen king someday, although it seemed like he would die before he saw that day. I am sure he remembered the day his father called him in from the pasture when Samuel was looking for him. I am sure he remembered walking into the house with all eyes on him, including all his brothers, who had just failed the test for king. And I am sure he remembered the feeling when Samuel poured oil on his head, anointing him king. What a thrill! Those were memories he would never forget and ones that helped him make it through each day. Remembering all the blessings of God is probably what kept him focused and sane when he thought he would literally go crazy running from his obsessive-compulsive father-in-law. When the devil tries to steal your victory, when he continually throws traps as you try to climb your mountain, remember your past experiences of God's faithfulness and remind him of his miserable future.

David talked about his valley, but he was not going to stay there. He was walking on through. I do not know why he wanted to walk. I would have used the word "run!" But it was not the Valley Of Death like we use so many times at funerals, it was the Valley Of The *Shadow* Of Death! It looked like he might die, but it was only a shadow. And what is it that must be present for a shadow to be made? Yes! You got it. Light! It was dark in that valley, but there was light in there, too. Where do you think the light came from? Right again! In your darkest night, look for the shadow, the positive shadow, because God has never left you, and He never will.

I decided to do an experiment with this. I got up early one morning when I was in St. Lucia and went to the pool. I stood in front of the sun, with my back to it, and looked into the crystal clear blue water. There was my shadow. I tried to do it the opposite way. I went to the other side of the pool and let the sun shine in front of me while I was facing it. No shadow. It was like God was saying, "I got your back! Just trust me and keep climbing."

There were several times over the past eleven years that I really thought I could die. The first time was when I was first diagnosed. I have taken care of cancer patients, have had friends who have had or have cancer, watched people go through chemo, and unfortunately, have attended many funerals of people who died because of cancer. I do not know about you, but when you hear a person has been diagnosed with cancer what are the first things that go through your mind? What kind of cancer is it, and how long do they have to live? And it seems like so many people are getting it, regardless of how young they are. When I was diagnosed by my first oncologist, confirming what my internist said, she was ready to start chemo and do a transplant ASAP. Your life pretty much passes quickly through your mind. You are not thinking about fighting at that point, you are wondering why, and how long, and this cannot be happening to me, and who will take care of my kids and my husband. And do not laugh, but you start seeing every single woman as a potential Mrs. Whitmire! The devil plays mind games with you any way he can. Of course you start planning your funeral. Just being honest. Can anyone relate to this?

Now fast forward my life a few years. The second time was three years ago when things were not looking too good again. My present oncologist from Siteman Cancer Center expressed that he felt it was time for me to have the dreaded stem-cell transplant. I had dug my heels in the dirt as long as he would let me. It was the procedure I did not want to go through. Here is a mini course about the procedure. First of all stem cells are immature blood cells in your body that eventually develop into the various types of mature blood cells. These are red blood cells, which carry oxygen, platelets, which help the blood clot, and white blood cells, which help fight infection. All of these cells are affected in multiple myeloma, because it is a disease of your bone marrow and all your blood cells are produced in your bone marrow. A stem cell transplant replaces defective or damaged cells in patients whose normal blood cells have been crowded out by cancerous cells.[31] In a typical stem cell transplant very high doses of chemo are used to try to destroy all of the cancerous cells. This treatment also kills the stem cells in the bone marrow. Soon after treatment, stem cells are given back to you to replace those that were destroyed. They are given back to you, through a port they insert into a large vein, much like a blood transfusion. Over time they settle in the bone marrow and begin to grow and make healthy blood cells. This process is called engraftment. I had an autologous stem cell transplant. In this type of transplant, your own stem cells are taken before you get the high doses of chemo that destroys the bad cells in your body. Your stem cells are removed, or harvested, from your blood and then frozen. After you get high doses of chemo, the stem cells are thawed and given back to you.[32] The port they use is inserted under anesthesia, which is another separate procedure, along with different medicines to allow your stem cells to be harvested more easily.

The day came for me to go for my transplant. It was so amazing how God works. Although I was praying I would be spared from that day, it was a weekend I will never forget. I was admitted to the hospital on Good Friday. Of all the weekends! I ruined it for a nice family holiday get together. What could possibly be good about today? But a few weeks prior I was talking to a hospital representative who must have been a Christian. She said, "I think it is the perfect weekend." I cringed. She said, "Good Friday did not look good to anyone either, but then Sunday came. Resurrection Day!" I thought about that, and that helped me put everything into a different perspective. I was literally going to die to my old immune system on Friday and then get my new one on Monday morning. God was going to bring me through this, but something had to die first. I was going to walk *through* the Valley Of The Shadow Of Death.

April 22, 2011

This is the day I thought would never come. Yet, I was filled with, as the Bible says, "a peace that passes all understanding." Of course I was supposed to get a good night's sleep. I did till 2:40 a.m. I hate those middle of the night calls you dread to answer, thinking it is going to be bad news. Instead, this was a call that I wanted to, at the least, hang up on. It was a couple who wanted us to extend their stay at the Budget Hotel. Didn't they know I was getting ready for the worst day of my life? Of course not.

Now I can't pack light. So of course Anita and Alhesha couldn't believe it and we couldn't fit my luggage in Alhesha's car. So we took half and Chuck took the other half. And as we were leaving Chuck said, "You're not going to the hospital, you're sneaking out and going on a cruise. I wish. Good old Chuck. He is an optimist at the highest level.

I am so thankful for good friends and a husband with a sense of humor. Three of my good friends drove me up to the hospital in St. Louis on Friday. Our first stop was Ruby Tuesdays. We all shared a meal together, before the big event, just like the "Last Supper." Of course I was praying it was not going to be. These ladies came up to decorate my hospital room. They asked me what theme I wanted and I decided I wanted encouraging scriptures plastered all over my walls. So they printed out scripture verses and put them all over my room, on my door, above my bed, and on every square inch of my room.

April 22, 2011

We had lots of laughs decorating my room with flowers, pictures of Jesus, and Bible verses. My nurse Julie said, "Wow, everyone is going to want to hang out in your room."

April 22, 2011

When I got to the hospital I had such a peace and joy in my heart. When the nurse came in the room, I was sitting on the bed and she looked at me, then Anita, then Alhesha, then Julie and asked, "Who is the patient?" She said, "You all look healthy."

After they decorated my room, we had a tearful goodbye. D day was coming later on that evening when I would get my first whopping dose of chemo. As my friends were leaving the hospital, my husband walked into my room with my son who just flew in from Indonesia to be with me for two weeks. Then it was a tearful hello.

April 22, 2011

I had to eat ice chips before my chemo at 9:00 p.m. (still am at 11:15 p.m.) to help with mouth sores. When 9:00 p.m. came I thought I would be nervous, but as the chemo went in, Chuck began to pray. My family and I all gathered in a circle—Nan Nan, Aimee, Chuck, Ryan, and me. That was the highlight of my day. Seeing Ryan. God keep your hand on him. He wants to go overseas again in 2012. Please, Lord, bring him back to you and provide him a helpmeet, if it is Your will. Touch him physically. Thank you for a good first day.

No matter what you are going through as a mother, your heart still worries about your children. You may think I am crazy for thanking God for a good first day when you know the circumstances surrounding the situation, but that is what I felt and that is what we have to do to get through our difficult situations.

I received my second heavy duty dose of chemo on Saturday. I rested on Sunday, Easter

Sunday, and received my transplant Monday morning. I was so thankful for my family and good friends.

April 23, 2011

Got up early. Listening to my "Transplant Tunes" Melanie (my daughter-in-law) made for me. Waiting for the family to get up. Last night was wild with tornadoes from here to Rolla and everywhere else. Sirens went off several times. Psalm 91:7 came to my mind. "A thousand may fall at your side, ten thousand at your right hand but it will not come near you." Keep the shield up Lord! Second and final dose of chemo. Hard to believe two days of half hour chemo. Feel pretty good. A little more tired than yesterday. RBC down and WBC up some. Walked ¾ mile.

Besides decorating my room with scriptures, I also decided to do an Easter theme. I filled a large basket, packing it with plastic Easter eggs. Each one was filled with candy and a Bible verse. My friend and prayer warrior, Jan, helped me fill them, and then we prayed over them. I had every doctor, nurse, aide, cleaning personal, lab technician, X-ray tech, and food service person take an egg and sign my guest book. It was amazing to lie in my bed and watch God's word make a difference in their lives.

My first night there, my first aide, took an egg. She was from China.

April 22, 2011

My first aide took an egg and came back and said that her egg had Filipino writing. Did I do that? She is from China. Maybe she got a verse from Philippians. God is good.

I prayed I would see her again so we could talk more about that. The next day she came into my room. That was the second day of my chemo.

April 23, 2011

I talked with my aide this morning. Four in the a.m. that is. I asked her about what she said about the Filipino writing? She said it was on her piece of paper. Praise God, it was from the book of Philippians. I showed her where it was in the Bible and gave her a Bible lesson, my testimony, and how faithful Jesus is all in five minutes. She said she did not have a Bible, so she was not familiar with it. I will believe and pray for her salvation!

Sunday was the day of rest for me. It was Easter, but my resurrection day would come tomorrow when I would get my stem cell transplant.

April 24, 2011

Missed going to church. Quiet day so far. Everyone went to church and out to eat. I am glad Ry went to church. Chuck took Nan Nan to Third Baptist Church where she used to go in the fifties. Had to get Lasix. Some shortness of breath and chest pain, but better now after Lasix. Gained a few pounds from fluids and will weigh later. Have had a weird "tic" (muscle spasms) in my neck and upper body. Chemo? No one seems interested in any of my complaints. Blame it all on the "chemo." So far I thank God how I feel. Will continue to believe for a miracle and minimal side effects.

Then the next really big day came. It was the day I got my stem cell transplant. I lost a day, so the next entry is the day after the transplant.

April 25, 2011

Missed a whole day. Nausea-vomiting. Although I felt sick from the N/V, I had no fear. Medication helped. Stem cells in two bags. First bag, minimal side effects. Tickle in throat, chest pressure. Second bag, fewer effects. Each bag took fifteen to twenty minutes. I couldn't keep my eyes open, so I must have been a sight. Those surrounding me: Chuck, Ryan, Aimee, Nan Nan, Anita, and Alhesha, along with God's presence.

The whole transplant procedure was so amazing. My stem cells were frozen in two bags. They came up frozen to my room in a small, normal-looking cooler, like you would take on a picnic. Only this was a picnic I would not want to go on again. Next, a specially trained transplant nurse took them out of the cooler and thawed them in the sink with running water, one bag at a time. When the first bag was thawed sufficiently, she quickly brought the bag of stem cells to my bedside and infused them into my bloodstream via my port. It had to be given as quickly as I could tolerate the side effects. The reason was thawed stem cells are very fragile and start dying very quickly after they are thawed. She then repeated the process with the second bag. That was the whole transplant procedure. It is quite amazing. Then we waited till my immune system revived. The chemo just about wipes out your whole immune system, especially your white blood cells, but your red blood cells and platelets are also affected. My lowest WBC reading was 0.1 which meant my body was very vulnerable to infection. After my stem cells were introduced back into my bloodstream, I had to wait till they did their job and began to find their way to make new and healthy blood cells in my bone marrow. That is why I had to stay in the hospital at least two weeks until that process began to happen. The only reason why I could have side effects from my own stem cells was due to the preservatives they put in the bags to keep the stem cells alive till I got my transplant. What was the weirdest thing about the whole procedure? Creamed corn. . .

April 25, 2011

My room smells like creamed corn from the preservative in my stem cells. Your lungs remove it from your body. I can't smell it but I won't be making creamed corn for a while.

What was really odd was I never could smell it, but everyone else could. Every time I exhaled, I infused my room with "essence of creamed corn." I am not sure how long it took everyone who was in the room that day to make creamed corn after the transplant. After that, every time I would take a walk around the floor, I knew exactly who was getting a transplant because I could smell the creamed corn odor as I passed their room.

One morning a new housekeeper walked into my room. I offered her an Easter egg, and she thanked me. The next day she came back into my room and said, "You made my day." She went on to explain. She said her three year old son's name was Jeremiah, and she got the verse from Jeremiah 29:11 in her egg. She explained that her son was going to a Christian Academy, and he was memorizing many of the verses from Jeremiah. God is so good!

Although I lay there, throwing up, hoping to make it to the bathroom in time because of Montezuma's Revenge, fighting nausea and weakness, and watching my hair fall out in clumps, I was amazed at the personnel with whom I had the opportunity to pray with, and the strength God gave me to minister. Nurses would come in and ask me my opinion for nursing situations. Cleaning ladies would come in and ask me to pray with them, pouring out to me their heart-wrenching stories. It was late the day I left to go home, because a cleaning lady wanted me to pray for her daughter who was struggling.

I almost did not want to leave the hospital. It doesn't matter what you are going through. Do not let the devil make you think that you cannot be used in a mighty way, regardless of how weak you think you are. I love that verse in II Corinthians 12:9 that says, "But he said to me, 'My grace is sufficient for you, for my power is made perfect in weakness. Therefore I will boast all the more gladly about my weaknesses, so that Christ's power may rest on me.'" Paul describes it perfectly, "My strength is made perfect in weakness." How can that be? It is only by the grace of God. Although it was a sobering thought spending the next two to three weeks in the hospital, God did "exceedingly abundantly above all I could ever imagine." It was so amazing to see, not only my family supporting me through the next few weeks and months to come, but friends who stepped up to the plate. I never spent the night alone. My son Ryan hardly left my side for two weeks, my other kids visited several times, and my friends Anita (my Barnabus) and Alhesha, took turns filling in staying at my bedside. I never was alone, humanly or divinely speaking.

I thank God for all my family who came to see me. All my kids came up one weekend, including the grandchildren, and some of Chuck's family. Not the best place for a family reunion but it lifted my spirit. We also have an "adopted son" Joe, who lived with us for a while, and is now part of our family. He just does not officially have the Whitmire name. He came for a surprise visit. It was like a small family reunion. Unfortunately, it was not under the best circumstances, but still a happy memory. I cannot tell you how many cards and letters I received from my church family and community. One day a staff person brought me a stack of cards, because that is how they usually came. She looked at me and said, "Are you famous or just popular? I have never seen anyone get so many cards."

As the transplant continued to do, what it was supposed to do, I felt like the Israelites felt the night the death angel passed through the streets of Egypt. I could imagine mothers holding their babies and fathers watching their first-born sleep, praying the death angel would see the blood on their door and pass over their dwelling. That is how I felt. People can die during a transplant from unforeseen complications or even from those that they know can potentially happen, but hope they don't. There were people physically dying on my floor, all around me, but I had God's Word pasted all over my door and walls, and God kept me safe. Revelation 12:11 says, "They triumphed over him by the blood of the Lamb and by the word of their testimony. . ." Death tried to make a dark shadow, but God had my back. He still does.

CHAPTER 13

Sometimes You Can Figure Things Out. Sometimes You Can't.

"I'm desperately trying to figure out why kamikaze pilots wore helmets."[33]

~ Dave Edison ~

Some things are just too complicated to figure out. Others just take a little determination. Did you ever figure out something that was way out of your league? Not only is it a shock to you and everyone around you, but it is also a very satisfying feeling. It gives you a sense of accomplishment. Let me share one of those moments with you. Let me preface it by saying I am not computer, iPhone, or iPad savvy. In other words, I am very illiterate in this area, so my illustration might make you laugh more than make my point! Or, if you are like me, you may be able to identify with the whole situation.

Since I have been in St. Lucia, it seems every time I go somewhere, I forget I can use my iPad to take pictures. It's sad, but true. It had been very overcast and rainy looking the last few days and since I will be leaving soon, I was thinking that I needed to take some last minute pictures. Everyone goes to bed early around here (meaning my son and his wife) so as the old saying goes, "If you can't beat 'em, join 'em." I went to bed last night at 9:00

p.m. That is early for me. I was going to read, but I left my Bible and books downstairs and I did not want to disturb anyone, so I went to sleep, eventually. Sunrise came early and it was so bright in my bedroom that I was wide awake at 5:30 a.m. This is so not me. It was a beautiful morning, so I decided to take my iPad with me for a walk to take pictures. I was so happy because I was getting some really great shots, but when I got back to the house to look at my pictures, to my horror, I had taken all videos. Oh no! Since it was still early I decided to do a déjà vu walk. Not a problem. Just switch it from video to picture. Right? Wrong. I could not get it to switch. I tried touching and sliding the camera icon to get it off video. Nothing. I restarted my iPad. Still set on video. I tried going into my settings, pretending I knew what I was doing, but still no luck. I was so frustrated. At this point I was so desperate that I called the reliable, toll-free, Apple support number, which is really an oxymoron. A very pleasant lady answered the phone, but gave me some very disturbing news. I did not have an extended warranty. I was only covered for ninety days and I was way past that. But not to worry, for a blue light special of $79.99, she would put me through to a technical support specialist who would solve my dilemma in no time. I thanked her and said I would try to figure it out myself. Yeah right. I started trouble shooting and turning buttons on and off, checking every few seconds if it worked. I tried looking at suggestions online, impatiently trying each one of them. And believe it or not, when I did the last whatever I did, it worked! Only I could not tell you now what I did to this very day. I went on my second walk and took pictures, although I could never reproduce the shots I did the first time to my complete satisfaction.

It is a great feeling when you can figure out something on your own, even if it is by accident. But life is not always like that. And neither is God. There are some things that are way out of our league and for those situations we must leave them in the hands of the only one who knows and sees the whole picture. But how hard is that? Very! Remember, heaven has the best technical support team there is, and God is the best trouble-shooter available. But do not forget, when you cannot see His hand . . . trust His heart!

CHAPTER 14

FAITH! WHAT IS YOUR COUNT?

"Faith isn't the ability to believe long and far into the misty future. It's simply taking God at His Word and taking the next step."[34]

~ Joni Erickson Tada ~

When you have cancer, you have to have your blood checked quite frequently, especially when your counts keep going the wrong way. I thank God for my doctor and nurses. They have been wonderful, but I also have the Great Physician, so I have an impressive team. Doctors do have a great deal of knowledge. But if you take away blood tests, bone marrows, MRI's, CAT scans, PET scans, X-rays, and medical books, they are unable to make a definite diagnosis for a serious illness. They can only make an educated guess, but they need to verify and confirm what they think with the results of the various tests they put you through to make a positive diagnosis. My doctor watches my blood work or "counts," to see the progression of the disease or the effectiveness of the medications they are administering. They always want to know what my numbers look like every month or so.

When you continue to have a prolonged illness and you routinely have to check your blood, you can tend to become obsessed with watching it every time it fluctuates, and it does fluctuate. Here is the scenario. You get your blood drawn, then you impatiently wait to hear the results, and depending on how they are, your treatment plan may change, you may have to adjust your medication, you may have to take a new drug, or you just repeat the same scenario and do the waiting game all over again. That was a mouth full.

When you are on chemo, doctors can judge whether the medication is working or not depending on certain markers that they look at. The bad thing is that you tend to become obsessed with the pattern of your blood work. You constantly are wondering if it is going to be good or bad this time around. Can you go another month without starting a whole new regime of treatment again? If the results are good, you feel great both mentally and physically, but if it is worse than the last time, even one-tenth of a point, it makes you feel anxious and physically exhausted. Trust me. It actually plays mind games with you.

It is really scriptural. Proverbs 15:20 says, "Light in a messenger's eyes brings joy to the heart, and good news gives health to the bones." I am trying to learn not to be obsessed with my blood work as much as I was in the beginning of this journey. I am not always successful . . . just ask my close friends. I used to call the nurse before my next appointment or check online for the results, but lately I just have been waiting and trying to trust God. For one thing, it could ruin my whole week if it is the slightest way wrong.

It is the same way with faith. What is your count? I mean spiritually speaking. What is your level of faith? On a scale of one to ten, say out loud what you think it is. No one is listening. Is this really important? Is it really vital to your spiritual health? Is it that important to your spiritual prognosis? Well, yes and no. I sound like a true politician. Sometimes people can become obsessive about levels of faith or talking about levels of faith. People may tell you that you do not have enough faith! Who measures it? How do you measure it? How much faith do you really need? These are interesting questions and ones that I have thought about quite a bit.

Remember in Matthew 21:21 Jesus replied, "Truly I tell you, if you have faith and do not doubt, not only can you do what was done to the fig tree, but also you can say to this mountain, 'Go, throw yourself into the sea,' and it will be done." How much faith do you need to do that? It has to be a lot, right? What did Jesus say in Matthew 17:20? "I tell you the truth, if you have faith as small as a mustard seed, you can say to this mountain, 'Move from here to there' and it will move. Nothing will be impossible for you." Wow! Remember how big an actual mustard seed is? Surely you have that much faith.

What about that dad in Mark 9:24? It says, "Immediately the boy's father exclaimed, 'I do believe; help me overcome my unbelief!'" And guess what? Jesus healed the father's son anyway. The dad who was struggling with unbelief! Are you kidding? You may think you do not have any faith, but FYI, God has given you faith. He has given every one of us faith. Look at Romans 12:3. "For by the grace given me I say to every one of you: Do not think of yourself more highly than you ought, but rather think of yourself with sober judgment, in accordance with the *faith* God has distributed to each of you." We all have faith that has been distributed to us, so what is the problem? The problem is sometimes we expect God to give us everything we ask for. If He does not give us what we want immediately, we think we have lack of faith or He did not hear us. I am sorry for you "name it and claim it people." I do believe in being persistent and bold when you prayer. Hebrews 14:6 says, "Let us then approach God's throne of grace with *confidence*, so that we may receive mercy and find grace to help us in our time of need." But . . .

Did you give your kids everything they asked for? What if they wanted candy for breakfast? Or what if they did not want to go to the dentist, or visit the doctor, or attend school? The answer is we did not give our children everything they wanted, because we loved them and wanted to do what was best for them. We knew what was best for them. Of course there were times our kids would ask over and over and say "please," "thank you," and "I love you." They finally wore us down, and then we gave in, but not every time. God is a loving father and, yes, we need to ask Him over and over just like that woman in Luke 18:4-5. It says, "For some time he refused. But finally he said to himself, 'Even though I don't fear God or care what people think, yet because this widow keeps bothering me, I will see that she gets justice, so that she won't eventually come and attack me!'" But that doesn't mean that we always get anything and everything we want. The bottom line is, God is faithful and just, and if it is in His will He will heal us, or deliver us, or give us what we are asking. But if He doesn't, He still is faithful and just.

My church just had an awesome prayer meeting for me tonight. Over sixty people on a Tuesday night. I was moved to tears and overwhelmed at how much my church loves me and wants me healed. I continue to believe God for a miracle. That is what I need. That is what I want. But if not, I will still serve Him and trust in His wisdom just like Daniel's friends. Their faith and trust in God was not based on if God was going to get them out of their situation or not. It was solely based on who God was, whether or not He delivered them. Oh, to have that kind of faith. Do not worry about what your faith count is, just make your faith count!

CHAPTER 15

Trust God No Matter What

"I believe in the sun when it's not shining, I believe in love even when I feel it not, I believe in God even when he is silent."[35]

~ Author unknown ~

I like the lyrics to Chris Tomlin's song, "I Will Follow." It says,

Where you go, I'll go.
Where you stay, I'll stay.
When you move, I'll move.
I will follow.[36]

God is ready to lead you, so where are you in this mountain climbing adventure? Are you motionless at the base, waiting for your mountain to move, or not quite sure of what you should do? Are you taking your first hesitant steps to try to climb it? Are you stuck in the middle wondering what to do next? Or are you on the summit looking at the beautiful view and shaking your head at the progress you have made, amazed how far God has brought you? Wherever you are, know there are many people in the same position as you.

Did you ever think the way God was leading you was crazy? I am sure that is what Joshua thought when God told him to have the Israelites circle the city of Jericho every day for six days, and then seven times on the seventh day. Did you ever think there is no way on earth you can do what He says. It just does not make sense, human sense, that is. But if you just step out in obedience you will find His ways are best.

I love the character of Moses. There are so many things I can relate to, minus killing a person, parting the Red Sea, or leading two million people out of Egypt. The part of the story I can relate to is how human this great man of God was. That is why I just love this story. Do you think Moses understood God's plan completely the first time he heard it? Moses tried so hard to get out of the assignment God was calling him to do. He used every excuse in the book, even after seeing three miracles: the burning bush, the rod that turned into a snake, and his own hand becoming leprous. Really, Moses? After all God did to convince him, he still did not want to do it. Why? Well, maybe because he felt inadequate, scared, and old. These are three really good reasons not to take the assignment. Can you imagine God calling you to lead two million people out of

Egypt, through the desert, at the age 80? Give him some slack for his excuses. I am sure Moses thought, "God, this cannot possibly work. It is too much for an old guy like me." But God was not convinced with his excuses. He said to Moses, "Don't worry. Your 83-year-old brother will help you." Wow, that would make me feel so much better. It is so hard to trust God when you cannot imagine what He is doing or how He is going to do it. Sometimes you just cannot see it happening at all.

I had a dream that I had forgotten. It was several months after my diagnosis, but it is so appropriate for this chapter.

August 18, 2003

I had a dream a few nights ago, where I was riding in a large vehicle with many people in it. I was in the passenger side of the front seat. The whole front was bricked where you could not see out anywhere. The brick was solid. I tried tapping at it. I commented to someone how hard it was to drive in a vehicle where you couldn't see. I glanced over to the driver who had a small window cut out; he looked very confident that he could see just fine. I sat back and relaxed, and we got to our destination. God was showing me He is in control and is in the driver's seat. Even though I can't see ahead at all, He wants me to trust Him to take me there. Oh God help me to have such faith!

I know sometimes it is easier said than done, but it makes things go so much better when we do not get stressed out and worry. God continues to help me every day. Do not think I always get it right. Just ask my friends, my husband, or my kids. It is okay to have a bad day or to stop for a pity party, just do not stay there. Life is not easy, and for some of us it is very hard. But in the midst of it all, I think one of the most important things to have in any trying, difficult situation, is a good sense of humor. I bet you were waiting for something profound, or even spiritual. Sorry. Even in the most challenging and scary situations you can find humor, even during the storm.

I have an entry to my journal that neither my husband nor I remember. It is not dated and must have been early in my diagnosis, but this is what it says:

Chuck real seriously asked where I wanted to be buried. I said in the back yard with our animals in our pet cemetery.

That may seem morbid to you but I think humor is so good for your overall health. I like what William Arthur Ward said, "A well-developed sense of humor is the pole that adds balance to your steps as you walk the tight rope of life." It is Biblical, too. Proverbs 17:22 says, "A merry heart does good, like medicine, but a broken spirit dries the bones." That's why I love the Bible. It is so practical and so spot-on. Solomon knew that fact nearly three thousand years ago. It took modern medicine a long time to confirm that. Laughter really is very healthy for you. Here are some things that actually happen when you laugh: It produces a reaction in the immune system which encourages good cell growth and suppresses damaging cell growth, including fighting cancer and tumor cells. It causes a reduction in stress hormones which constrict blood vessels and hinder immune activity. It provides aerobic exercise. No more going to the gym for me. It is said that hearty laughter can burn calories comparable to several minutes on the rowing machine or the exercise bike. It causes muscle relaxation, first to the muscles not involved in the laugh, then a tensing and relaxation of those involved in laughing. It releases endorphins. That is one of the body's natural pain killers. Time to stop taking the NSAIDS. It also showed that laughing encourages both right and left side brain activity which enhances learning, reduces tension, and adds to the brain's alertness and its ability to retain information.[37] So go read some good jokes or put on your Mark Lowry videos.

The other day I got a startling phone call from Steve, my daughter-in-law's father. What would he be calling me about? He calmly said that they had to bring Melanie, my daughter-in-law, to the ER because she had a severe asthma attack. This is the second time she has done this. The family started praying. A few hours passed and I got a phone call. It was

Melanie and she obviously was feeling better, although it was a very terrifying experience for her and the family.

I asked her how the kids did through all this. She said Marek, my five year old grandson, was crying when it all started happening, but after the medical personnel got her stabilized and were wheeling her out he smiled and said, "Thanks guys for coming." We all got a good laugh at that one.

I had a sign-in book during my transplant procedure, and I was looking at what people wrote. Most of the entries were serious but here are a few that still make me laugh.

Dear Annette,

Get well quickly—I can't afford to share my brain with you much longer! Love you, Alhesha

Here was what my children wrote:

Ryan Whitmire - Devoted son
Tyler Whitmire – Prodigal Son

Aimee Whitmire – Best all-around
Kyle Whitmire – Best looking son

Seriously, trust God no matter what is happening or where He is taking you. Sometimes the journey is a long one, but instead of wondering where He is taking you, ask what you can do to be a witness along the way. I remember my very first bone marrow procedure. I have had over twenty! I went up the night before to spend the night in a hotel, because it was going to be early and the hospital was an hour-and-a-half drive away. Two of my friends came up to support me. I remember I had a hard time falling asleep, but I finally did. I woke up in the middle of the night, and my eyes were drawn to the door frame. I rubbed my eyes because I thought I was seeing things. I looked back and there above the door frame was a lamb. That was odd. I turned away and looked up again, and the scene changed. The Good Shepherd was now holding the lamb. I began to weep. I looked up again, but the scene was gone. From the very beginning God was telling me He would take care of me and carry me through. He never gave me any details, but just told me that I just needed to trust and follow and let Him carry me when and where I need Him to.

The next morning was my first bone marrow procedure. God was in that room, too.

August 11, 2003

I was being prepped. I was on the seventh floor and my room had two sevens in it. I thought, "That's a good sign (silly)." When I was being prepped and almost ready for the stick, I said, "Wait a minute. Are any of you praying people?" There was silence for a second or two, and then the nurse at the foot of my bed said in a clear, low voice, "I'm with you." Then the nurse next to me in a low, quiet, voice said, "I believe in prayer too." I said, "I didn't hear anything from the doctor." It took him a few seconds and then he said, "I am a man of faith. I will believe too."

Honestly, you can find God anywhere you go. You can be used in every situation you face. God will never leave you, so trust Him no matter what.

CHAPTER 16

FALLING UP

"The greatest glory in living lies not in never falling, but in rising every time we fall."[38]

~ Nelson Mandela ~

Almost every time I hear people use the word "falling" it is associated with the word "down." For example, "I fell down the stairs." You usually do not fall up the stairs, unless you are extremely uncoordinated. I was visiting a church with my daughter-in-law's parents, and the title of their pastor's sermon caught my attention. It was called, "Falling Up." I was intrigued by the title. After listening to the message, it seemed to be a perfect fit for my book, and so began the creation of another chapter. Pastor Kevin Glenn of Memorial Baptist Church in Columbia, Missouri, preached a great sermon on not letting fear and failure keep us frozen in a place where we cannot make any progress forward. And that is what your situation can do to you if you will let it. It will not only keep you from going forward, but can actually make you go backwards. If you are going to fall, at least fall up! Fall forward. You may not think you are making progress but you are. At least you are not going backwards. Fear can do that to you. We all are afraid of something. I am afraid of flying insects, snakes, roaches, and heights. These are on my top ten list. What is your biggest fear?

One morning I woke up and went into the kitchen to eat breakfast, as I usually do. I was in that semi-conscious state. I walked into the kitchen and stopped dead in my tracks. My first thought was that my husband was playing a terrible practical joke on me. You have to know my husband. He is the king of practical jokes and sometimes he goes too far. There, in front of me was a snake in the coiled position. It looked just like the ones you buy at the dollar store. There was no way it could be real. Could it? At this point I was not quite convinced either way, but just in case, I ran downstairs and got a broom. Wow, great thinking. Now when I reflect back, I realize that probably was not the best thing to do, but it did turn out okay. I also picked up a ten pound weight from the garage. At this point my adrenaline was in control. I ran back up the stairs and found it in exactly the same position. It had not moved one millimeter. I am not sure why I did this. I guess I was thinking it was a fake snake, or at least hoping it was.

I got real close to look at it. No movement. Then impulsively I shoved the reptile with the broom in one sweeping motion and watched it glide across the hardwood floor still coiled in the same position. For a split second I was mad. "It is a fake snake. He knows how I hate snakes. That is so mean." And then I saw it. A slight movement of the head and then it started to sluggishly uncoil. It started picking up speed and tried to slither away down the hall to the nearest dark closet. I could not believe this was happening to me. For a split second I was frozen, but I knew I had to kill it, or I would have to move out of my home until someone else did. I took the 10lb weight, held it above its body and let it fall on one of my biggest fears. The whole body coiled up again and fit perfectly under the weight, but its head kept rising up. "Please God don't let it get loose!" I prayed that out loud. Reflecting back now, I think I was shaking. Then I did the grossest, most impulsive thing I have ever done, and stepped on the weight with as much force as my wobbly legs could muster. Every time I stepped on the weight that little head with beady eyes would pop up and it would open its mouth as wide as it would go as if to say, "I wish I could bite you for what you are doing to me. You better pray I don't get loose."

Then I got another brilliant idea. I spotted my tall jar of pennies I had been saving for a mission's project. It had to be at least ten pounds. I know now there was a reason why it took so long to fill it. I picked it up and dropped it on its head and heard the slight crunching sound of tiny little bones breaking. And I immediately thought of that verse in Genesis 3:15 that says, "He will crush your head, and you will strike his heel."

This just reinforced to me that Satan has already been defeated. There is no problem or sickness that can destroy you. Satan may try to frighten you with his scare tactics. He may grab at your feet to knock you over or make you fall, but Christ has already crushed his head. He is not more powerful than the power of Christ in you. If we will see every problem like that despicable snake, we can be victorious every time. It is hard to face your fears. It was so hard for me to get close enough to that snake to crush it. I knew if I did not face one of my greatest fears I would have an even bigger problem: a loose snake in my house.

Ambrose Redmoon said, "Courage is not the absence of fear."[39] It is not even about eliminating your fears. It is about pressing on when your knees shake. And mine were. Eddie Rickenbacker, the World War II flying ace, said it well, "Courage is doing what you're afraid to do. There can be no courage unless you're scared."[40] Pastor Glenn also said, "Run towards your fears or they will pursue you."[41] Just like that snake that tried to slither away. I had to chase it. I had to run towards it. I had to take control of it. Whether it is killing a snake, overcoming your worst fear, or climbing your most treacherous mountain, do not let fear freeze you. Let it fuel you to keep climbing. But if you happen to fall, fall up!

CHAPTER 17

I WANT TO LIVE WITH ABANDON!

"You only live once, but if you do it right, once is enough."[42]

~ Joe Lewis ~

Do you ever wake up with a song in your head and in your heart? I do quite often, and I did this morning. I do not know what I would do without Christian music. There are times that I just cannot function for the day. I hate to admit this, but there are days when I cannot pray or read my Bible. I just can't focus. But I can find my favorite radio station and crank up the music, and it can usher me into God's presence in a few seconds. It never ceases to amaze me how the right song with the right words will come on the radio at just the right time. You probably got the song in your head when you saw the title to this chapter. It is "Live With Abandon" by the Newsboys. Live with who? Some people live with depression or unforgiveness. Others live with difficult spouses or unbearable situations, but I want to live with abandon.

I wanna live with abandon.
Give You all that I am.
Every part of my heart Jesus
I place in Your hands.[43]

What does abandon mean? According to Merriam-Webster, it means to leave and never return to; to give oneself over unrestrainedly.[44] That is how I want to live my life for God. That is how we all should live, and they say it so well. Whatever is holding you back, blocking your path, or making you feel trapped, let it go! Whatever mountain is in your way, start climbing and do not look back, except to learn from your mistakes. Never ever go back. Always push forward, even if it is only a small step and you think you are not making any progress. You are if you are not going backwards.

Little steps add up to big ones. A penny is the smallest amount of money, but if you have a lot of them you could have a lot of money. Most people might see a penny on the ground and leave it there, but I always pick it up. My mom showed me the value of a penny as a child. We did not have a lot of money growing up, but we saved all our pennies in a jar for the missionaries, and it did add up. It was such a rewarding feeling to put all those pennies in a penny roll and take them to the bank. Then we would take the cash to church with us and put the money in an envelope designated "missions." Remember the old saying, "Take care of the pence and the pounds will take care of themselves?"[45] It was first quoted by the Secretary of the Treasury, Mr. William Lowndes who was born in 1652. It means if you take care of the little things one at a time, they can add up to big things. It is the same with climbing your mountain. If you move forward with little steps, someday you will look back and see how far you have come. Trust me on this one. You can do it, one baby step at a time!

I have a pedometer I use when I walk. I try to walk one or two miles down my road and back several times a week. Well, that was several months ago when I was not taking my "new" chemo and had a bit more energy than I do now. On the little package the pedometer came in, it encouraged you to walk 10,000 steps a day. That's a lot of steps! Are you kidding me? At first it seemed impossible. How can anyone possibly do that many steps? But I decided to at least try it. I walked my normal two miles down my driveway with the little device attached to my sock. It went everywhere with me. Up and down my steps to the basement doing laundry, going from room to room making beds, picking up dirty clothes, and going grocery shopping. To my surprise, by the end of the day, I had walked 10,000 steps! Actually 10,000 steps is only about five miles. That's what I mean when I say take one baby step at a time because they do add up. You can do it!

I was sitting in church one Sunday morning and the song leader started singing the song, "10,000 Reasons (Bless the Lord)" by Matt Redman. That is ten thousand reasons to bless the Lord. Of course, I started crying. I thought about that. Maybe that is a slight exaggeration, but there are so many reasons why we should thank the Lord for all the blessings in our life. If you start counting them, they too, will add up to more than you could ever imagine.

"The sun comes up, it's a new day dawning
It's time to sing Your song again

Whatever may pass, and
whatever lies before me
Let me be singing when the evening comes"[46]

I do have bad days but my goal is to "be singing when the evening comes" one baby step at a time.

CHAPTER 18

WHEN IT RAINS IT POURS

"Anyone who says sunshine
brings happiness has never
danced in the rain."[47]

~ Author Unknown ~

"Everybody wants happiness, nobody
wants pain, but you can't have a
rainbow without a little rain."[48]

~ Author Unknown ~

Did you ever feel that way? What I mean is sometimes when one thing goes wrong, a lot of things go wrong at the same time. It just does not rain problems, it pours problems. An umbrella works fine for light rain and no wind, but in a hurricane, it just will not cut it. A few problems you can handle. A flat tire, you did not know you had a run in your panty hose, you wore two wrong-colored shoes to church, someone told you if you brought a banana to McDonald's you would get a free meal, and maybe you even ran out of gas. And by the way, all of these have happened to me, but not all in one day. That would be a bit harder to manage. I really did fall for the banana thing. It was very embarrassing. Take a few small problems or just everyday life with your family and then throw in a few more, like struggling with cancer for eleven years, having to stop chemo, which your doctors say you desperately need, because of an allergic reaction you had to it, your healthy husband goes to ER with chest pain and shortness of breath, you have a son who has gone from doctor to doctor for severe stomach issues and has no rest from the pain and anxiety associated with it, you are up all night with leg cramps that are worse than labor pains, you are trying to be a mother, a grandmother, and a pastor's wife, and you are trying to do all of this with a hemoglobin of 8.7 and falling. All in one twenty-four-hour day! And that was just today. You may say, "That's nothing. You should hear my story!" We all have days we would rather not have to deal with. The problem is they do not just last a day. They turn into weeks, months, and years! Sometimes it is so hard to keep a positive attitude when your trial is like the Energizer Bunny.

Right now I am sitting in a doctor's office waiting for the cardiologist to figure out why my strong fifty-four-year-old husband who swims three times a week, and preaches four, is short of breath. But it is so hard to concentrate on him when I am wondering what is going to happen to me. Ever been there? Makes you feel extremely guilty and immensely human. My oncologist started me on a chemo pill a few days ago. A pill that he said most people tolerate well without any severe side effects. That is everyone, except me.

Last night my husband and I were driving down the highway in a snow storm for his echocardiogram test scheduled for today, and I had an allergic reaction to my chemo pill. The one most people tolerate so well. Not only that, but I have been having this unexplained facial numbness like I just had a Novocain shot to extract my tooth, only I really didn't. I debated whether to go to the ER but decided to take a Benadryl and call my doctor in the morning. After talking with the doctor, I had to stop my chemo and live on Benadryl for a few nights in a hotel away from home, till my husband completed all his tests. My oncologist wanted me to come up to see him as soon as possible, but I cannot because St. Louis, Missouri, is in the opposite direction of Columbia, Missouri, where we are headed and I need to be with my husband. After a restless night in an uncomfortable hotel bed, I sit here waiting to talk with my husband's doctor with a Benadryl hangover, trying to focus on him and not worry about me. I am sure you can relate with similar situations in your life.

If my mom were alive today she would be quoting that verse in I Corinthians 10:13, "No temptation has overtaken you except what is common to mankind. And God is faithful; He will not let you be tempted beyond what you can bear. But when you are tempted, He will also provide a way out so that you can endure it." Sometimes I dislike that verse or verses like that. But let's take a closer look at what it is really saying.

The Greek word for temptation is "peirasmos." This Greek word for temptation and tempted can also mean testing and tested. It not only can mean a temptation to sin but a proving trial.[49] So what does "proving" mean? It means to subject to a test, experiment, comparison, or analysis to determine quality, amount, or acceptability. It is to show oneself to have the character or ability expected of one, especially through one's actions.[50] Wow! I love what Mother Theresa said, "I know God will not give me anything I can't handle. I just wish

He didn't trust me so much."[51] Did you ever feel like that? If you are having a bit of trouble enduring your situation, maybe you should try changing your attitude or just try to have an "attitude adjustment." I heard it said, "Attitude is the little thing that makes a big difference."

We decided to have "Home Church" one Sunday that my husband was on vacation. My daughter chose to go to "real" church and two of our boys and our daughter-in-law attended home church with us. We gathered around the kitchen table. No one wanted to sing a special and taking an offering was vetoed by the congregation, so my husband just started doing what he loves to do best, preach.

His sermon was titled, "Grasshoppers Don't Eat Grapes." I do not know if that was original or not, but you might guess what it was about. It was taken from the sad account of the twelve spies who had just spent forty days looking over the Promised Land. The land flowing with milk and honey and giants! It is found in Numbers 13 and it would be beneficial to you if you took the time to read it, because it is so applicable to life and the giants we may face in our lives. Sometimes we get so critical of those ten faithless leaders; yes, they were leaders of the twelve tribes! No ordinary men, but men chosen by Moses, at God's command, as the cream of the crop. All twelve men saw the same thing. They all spent the same amount of time spying out the land together. They all were leaders the Israelites looked up to, hand-picked by Moses. What happened to these great men of God? It is the same thing that happens to us. They chose to let their circumstances paralyze them into missing out on God's greatest blessing in their lives. But their choices not only affected them, their choices affected the whole Israelite community.

Thus, the choices we make not only have repercussions on our life, but on the lives of those we influence, or even those we do not know we are influencing. It is like the ripple effect when you throw a pebble into the water and watch the ripples form. "The ripple effect is a direct effect that spreads out from the direct or main effect to reach areas or population far removed from its intended or original purpose or target."[52] Sometimes the consequences of our choices go further than we could ever imagine without us even knowing.

Grasshoppers will never eat grapes. They cannot eat grapes because they have a negative attitude about life and what God can do. They veto anything that God wants to do in their life because they are paralyzed by their circumstances, and by fear. If you have a grasshopper mentality then you will have a hard time reaping the benefits God has for you. For the Israelites it was grapes and other produce from the land, plus an awesome place to live. Better than the desert for sure. Their attitude and influence affected not only their lives, but the lives of a whole nation, and, sadly, their own children. It's the same way in our lives. As parents, whether we realize it or not, we are influencing our children, either negatively or positively. The old saying, "Do as I say, not as I do" does not cut it. We need to ask God to help us be the example He wants us to be. If you made some mistakes with your children, then make changes and be the spiritual example God wants you to be with you grandchildren.

Now here is another interesting thought I want to share with you. We always hear it preached that if something is God's will then all the doors and windows will swing wide open and a huge flashlight from heaven will shine on your path and God will say, "Whether you turn to the right or to the left, your ears will hear a voice behind you, saying, 'This is the way; walk in it.'" That is in Isaiah 30:21. Yes it can be done that way. Obviously, God has done it that way in the past, and He still could do it that way in the future. Unfortunately, that is not always the way He does it, at least not routinely in an audible voice. But I would like to tell you a true story about God speaking to a woman in a miraculous way that is hard to believe, but absolutely true.

There was a young woman who was very newly saved. God radically transformed her and then delivered her from smoking, drinking, cussing, gambling, and various other vices she needed to be delivered from. She was alone one night, because her husband was working late. She never liked being alone. In fact she got pretty fearful when she had to stay alone. She prayed to God to watch over her and keep her safe and then tried to fall asleep. Suddenly she heard an audible voice, "Your keys are in the kitchen door." For a minute she panicked. She lay there hoping she was imagining hearing the voice. I could picture her pulling the blankets over her head as tightly as she could. Well, maybe not that tight because she was also claustrophobic. Again the voice said, "Your keys are in the kitchen door." She said the voice sounded like rushing waters. After a while it finally dawned on her that the voice was "The Lord" speaking to her. Although she was terrified at the thought of God talking to her, she nonetheless started arguing with Him and said, "No the keys are on top of the refrigerator." That is where she always kept them every night. Without warning she jumped up out of bed, as if she were being pushed, and ran immediately to the kitchen and straight to the refrigerator.

She confidently said, "See Lord, they are right here," as she frantically checked the top of the refrigerator. But all she found was dust. They were not there. That was impossible. She ran to the front door, unbolted the dead bolt, and to her horror and then relief, she noticed that she had forgotten her keys in the door. This took place in a New York City apartment building late at night. She quickly removed the keys from the keyhole, flung them on top of the refrigerator where they belonged, jumped into bed with the covers hiding her face, and said a quick, "Thank you, Lord!" I know this is a true story because that lady was my mom. I remember the keys were always on top of the refrigerator growing up. I do not even think she knew of that verse in Revelation 1:15 at that time that says, "His feet were like bronze glowing in a furnace, and his voice was like the sound of rushing waters." I think the funniest part was her arguing with God. And we criticize Moses? But don't we all do the same thing in different ways?

As I was listening to my husband's sermon at home church, another thought popped into my head. It definitely was God's will for the children of Israel to conquer the land the first time, but there were huge obstacles in their way, mainly giants and "The Great Wall Of Jericho." I believe God wanted them to see the obstacles, yet choose to trust Him, knowing that He was greater than any obstacle. They just could not get passed the hurdle. Didn't they remember the ten plagues and how the death angel passed over every firstborn son of Israel? Didn't they see Moses part the Red Sea and watch all the Egyptians drown? What about when Moses threw a piece of wood into the waters of Marah to make it sweet? And didn't He bring water from a rock and provide enough manna and quail for the entire nation to eat for a long time? We are not talking about feeding the 5,000 for one day.

What was wrong with them? Probably the same thing that is wrong with us. We do the same thing. We look at the obstacles and think God does not want us to go forward. We forget what He has done for us in the past. It is so interesting to hear the report of those negative spies in Numbers 13:27-33.

"They gave Moses this account. 'We went into the land to which you sent us, and it does flow with milk and honey! Here is its fruit. But the people who live there are powerful and the cities are fortified and very large. We even saw descendants of Anak there. The Amalekites live in the Negev; the Hittites, Jebusites and Amorites live in the hill country; and the Canaanites live near the sea and along the Jordan.' Then Caleb silenced the people before Moses and said, 'We should go up and take possession of the land, for we can certainly do it.' But the men who had gone up with him said, 'We can't attack those people; they are stronger than we are.' And they spread among the Israelites a bad report about the land they had explored. They said, 'The land we explored devours those living in it. All the people we saw there are of great size. We saw the Nephilim there (the descendants of Anak come from the Nephilim). We seemed like grasshoppers in our own eyes, and we looked the same to them.'"

Unfortunately they did not see the situation like God saw it. They did not even see it like the Canaanites saw it. Now fast forward this story about forty years. Look at Joshua 2:8-11:

"Before the spies lay down for the night, she (Rahab) went up on the roof and said to them, 'I know that the Lord has given you this land and that a great fear of you has fallen on us, so that all who live in this country are melting in fear because of you. We have heard how the Lord dried up the water of the Red Sea for you when you came out of Egypt, and what you did to Sihon and Og, the two kings of the Amorites east of the Jordan, whom you completely destroyed. When we heard of it, our hearts melted in fear and everyone's courage failed because of you, for the Lord your God is God in heaven above and on the earth below.'"

Wow! The Canaanites, an ungodly nation, realized how powerful the God of Israel was. They were scared of the Israelites from the very first miracle God performed when they first left Egypt, the parting of the Red Sea. It only took one miracle for them to believe. How many miracles did the Israelites see? How sad. The crazy thing was that they were still talking about it forty years later! How many things do you remember from forty years ago? You usually just remember the important ones. It is the ones that really made an impact on your life. If the Israelites knew this little bit of information, would their attitude have been different the first time they spied out the land? They probably could have skipped wandering in the dessert for forty years. Makes you wonder.

If we would only learn to trust God no matter what we see with our natural eyes, things might turn out differently in our lives. What are you scared of? What is paralyzing you? What situation are you stuck in? Maybe you need to take a closer look. What you may think is a roadblock may be God saying, "Move forward and trust me!" When it pours, forget the umbrella or trying to do it your way, and let God use His power to bring you through the storm His way.

CHAPTER 19

Pray For Me And I'll Pray For You

"Groanings which cannot be uttered are often prayers which cannot be refused."[53]

~ Charles Spurgeon ~

"Is prayer your steering wheel or your spare tire?"[54]

~ Corrie Ten Boom ~

Notice everything I say reminds me of a song? Well, if you lived with my husband you would see why I am like this after thirty four years of marriage. Anything you say, he turns into a song. It is really hard to converse with him at home, especially if you are in a bad mood, which is very rare. He does it spontaneously during the middle of his sermons too. Only sometimes he gets the words wrong. I found this song. I have never heard it sung before, but I love the lyrics.

"Can I Pray For You" by Mark Bishop

I've been your friend for a while.
I know you're hiding behind that smile,
And you're keeping inside tears
that should have been cried,
You've been brave through this trial.
You've been as strong as a stone,
Against the stormy winds that have blown.
But you have friends who care,
more than willing to share,
Don't face those troubles alone.

Chorus:
Can I pray for you?
Can I mention your name to the Lord?
When I seek His face, can I plead your case?
That's what praying is for.
I'll help you carry your cross,
And find the way when you're lost.
If we'll let Jesus be true, I know
that He'll see you through.
Can I pray for you?

I know that there'll come a day.
When I'll have trials and need you to pray.
Just like you've done before, you'll
mention me to the Lord,
That's why I'm here to say:
"Let me be there for you.
We'll divide all your problems by two.
And very soon there'll be three
– you and Jesus and me.
That's what friends are supposed to do."

If we'll let Jesus be true, I know
that He'll see you through.
Can I pray for you? [55]

Have you ever said to someone, "I'll be praying for you?" Or has someone asked you to pray for them? Do you always follow through with it? If I can share one thing with you in this short chapter, it is this: If you tell someone you are going to pray for them, then do it. How many times have you had good intentions, but the next time you see that person it hits you that you did not keep your word. People depend on your prayers. People's lives depend on your prayers. Prayer can move the heart of God.

I collect a lot of things in my house from Noah's Arks to Nativities, but my favorite collection is prayers. Every time a strong pray warrior dies I feel like I am a little more vulnerable. My all-time favorite prayer warrior died on March 16, 2013, the day before my birthday. It was the worst birthday ever because she was my mom. Not only did she pray for me every day, but throughout the day and night. I know that for a fact, because she told me. She did not sleep well during the night, so she would pray for me all night long sometimes and I miss her and her prayers. But God is so faithful! When He takes someone to be with Him who has been praying for me, it seems God brings another person into my life to fill that void. I have people literally praying for me from California to the New York Islands and around the world. I know that is what keeps me going.

I knew my church family and my relatives were praying for me, but I never realized how many people were praying for me in my community. I could be in a grocery store or my husband visiting someone in the hospital, and a new prayer warrior would be revealed.

January, 16, 2004

It never ceases to amaze me how many people are praying for me, still. People I do not even know. Like yesterday, Chuck was in the hospital and two women were walking together. The younger said, "How's Annette?" Chuck said, "She is doing okay." The older lady said, "Is that Annette Whitmire?" Chuck said, "Yes." She said, "I don't get to go to church, but

I pray for her every day!" Chuck did not know either lady. Wow.

I could be at Walmart or eating out at one of our local restaurants and there is hardly a time when someone doesn't come up to me and ask how I am and say, "I am praying for you." This may seem silly, but I like to play scrabble online. One of my opponents is a lady who I first met at a yard sale I had at my house years ago. We have been friends for years. We sometimes chat during our scrabble games. One day she asked how I was, and then she told me, "I pray for you every day." It brought tears to my eyes. I had no idea.

I also have that wonderful lady in church who is my personal prayer warrior. She has had her share of difficulties, and her health has not always been the best. She has had many trials in her life, yet God has placed me on her heart. That is the one who started six weeks of intensive prayer after my transplant. Six weeks of prayer every day in my house and in church on Sunday. As I had mentioned earlier, she got together a special corporate time of prayer for me. There was an email sent out to our church that there was going to be a special prayer meeting on a Tuesday night. I was trying so hard to be there, but I developed a fever. She did the next best thing. She called me and had the phone on speaker. It was amazing. Over sixty people gathered on a Tuesday night for their pastor's wife. Both men and women were weeping in their pews or at the altar. It was such a humbling experience. All I could do was close my eyes and inhale each prayer that was prayed, straining to hear the words they were saying to our Father for me. I sat there in my recliner at home and wept. My son stayed home with me and bowed his head with his hand on me. It was one of the most emotional experiences of my life. That is what the church is supposed to be. This is the church at its finest hour. I am blessed. Thank you for praying for me.

CHAPTER 20

BE STRONG

"If we desire our faith to be strengthened, we should not shrink from opportunities where our faith may be tried, and therefore, through trial, be strengthened."[56]

~ George Mueller ~

I hope I have helped even just one person along in their journey. I do not know where you are in your mountain climbing experience. Maybe you are still at the bottom of your mountain looking up at it, wondering what to do next. Maybe you started and you are already sitting down on the first rock you can find, feeling discouraged. Maybe you have tripped and have your face to the ground thinking, "I can't do this!" Maybe you are making some good progress and just need an, "Atta girl, keep going." Or maybe you are stuck in a place where the road is narrow and winding and you cannot see around the next bend. Don't ever give up! Maybe you are saying, "I almost have this licked!" Or maybe you have pushed your mountain into the sea! Hallelujah! I would love to hear your stories.

In case you are lost on the trail, let's take a quick look at our road map, the Bible, and see if we can pull this all together and keep you climbing. The Bible is God speaking to us words of encouragement, conveying to us that we can make it, but not all in the same way! For the children of Israel, God used Moses to part the Red Sea. Then God used Joshua to push back the Jordan's flood waters. But Shadrach, Meshach, and Abednego had to go through the fire. Daniel spent the night in "The Lion's Den and Suites." Please read Hebrews 11. We would all love to have our names in the first part of the chapter where all the great men of God are listed for their acts of faith. Wouldn't you want your name in there? But the second part of the chapter is another Hall of Fame listing of all those great men and women of God who died horrible martyr's deaths. And of course God raised Lazarus from the dead, but unfortunately he had to die again. God is in control. It is too bad we are so human and life causes us to get stressed out at times. No matter what the situation you are in, you have to go through it. Either kicking and screaming, or trusting God.

My husband is an avid reader. His goal is to read a book a month, on top of preaching four times a week, plus everything else a pastor does. And he reads big books like *Bonhoeffer*, by Eric Metaxas. Have you seen the size of that book? Not like the books I used to read. He calls them "Christian Soaps" in a book. Good books written by Jeanette Oak or Grace Livingston Hill. I used to read a lot, and they are great stories, but I have not read much for the past five or six years. He is challenging me to read a book a month, but I have a hard enough time just reading my Bible and writing this book.

Maybe you cannot read through the Bible, but it does not matter whether it is a verse, a chapter, or a book, just start. It is so important to keep God's word in our hearts and mind. It is our strongest tool against our enemy. That's what Jesus used against the devil, and the devil could not stand against the Word of God.

My good friend and author, Carol Hudler, gave me a book for Christmas written by Warren W. Wiersbe, called *Be Strong.* It is about the life of Joshua. Wiersbe says in his book, "The book of Joshua is the book of new beginnings for the people of God, and many believers today need a new beginning."[57] This may be your day of new beginnings. This may be the year to take a risk. A time to trust God and conquer your biggest fears in a way you have never done before. Do not look back and be discouraged, but look forward and be encouraged because with God's help you can do it.

And thank God he gives us a Barnabus to help us. Who was Barnabus? Act 4:36 says he was, "Joseph, a Levite from Cyprus, whom the apostles called Barnabas (which means "son of encouragement"). The Greek word is paraklēsis. It means consolation, comfort, solace; that which affords comfort or refreshment."[58] I have a few encouragers, but one especially who has been there for me for many years, quietly in the background. She calls me or texts me almost every day to see how I am. And if she does not like the way I sound in the morning, she will call in the afternoon, just in case. It has been hard for me to receive help these last few years, because I am a giver and have always tried to be strong for everyone else. But now it is my turn to be on the receiving end, and I struggle.

I just finished a book called, *Seeing Beyond,* by Gail McWilliams. It is an encouraging book to the awesome power of God's grace, mercy, and protection. It is amazing how what she wrote is exactly what I feel. A friend of mine told me when she read her book she thought about me. Here is a paragraph that fits here so well. "It is humbling to be vulnerable to others. I wondered if I had any value. I no longer felt like the life-giver, only the energy drainer. How could I help my husband? How would I completely care for my little girl and her growing needs? I had an unlimited faith for Anna's hopeless situation, but I lacked faith for my own predicament."[59] I felt like we were kindred spirits. She also went on to say later in her book, "In some situations and on many days, I, too, have been tempted to give up. Then I ask myself, 'Give up to what, and to whom?' At first, it was hard for me to ask for help. At times it is still frustrating to have to share my journey with others that must come alongside to assist me. It is very humbling not to appear perfect and perhaps to be vulnerable. Trust enables you to take one more step, knowing that you don't have to see the end of the road. Determination is the backbone to stay in the race. Finishing well is the prize."[60] Amen, Sister Gail!

Thank you to all who have come alongside of me and helped me to keep going when I did not want to. I wish I could list all the names of everyone who has helped carry my load these past eleven years but that would fill another book. So many people have helped me in so many ways, from cleaning my house to organizing my closet with all new clothes hangers. Thank you all for having patience with me during all my "Debbie Downer Days."

My parting words to you are "be strong." Be strong, stay strong, and most of all, finish strong. God gave me this poem during my teenage years when I thought the whole world was caving in on me.

Your Trials Come To Only Make You Strong

The skies look overcast and stark.
The storm seems very near.
The clouds are very bleak and dark.
Your heart is filled with fear.

Your faith is growing very weak
And God seems far away.
The night is all around.
You long for light of day.

You feel that you are lost
You drop down to your knees.
The winds are strong and raging.
It's very hard to see.

You're being tossed and driven.
But in the dark you hear
A still small voice that's saying,
"My precious child, I'm here."

And soon you see a glimpse of light.
Though very hard to see.
Again you hear that voice.
"Child I'm near to Thee."

The light is getting brighter.
Your faith is growing strong.
The storm is passing over.
Within you have a song.

The winds are slowly calming.
You feel a gently breeze.
You lift your eyes toward heaven,
Upon your bended knees.

Again you hear that Voice
That you've waited for so long.
"My child I send you trials,
Just to make you strong."

CHAPTER 21

Great Is Thy Faithfulness

"Often times God demonstrates His faithfulness in adversity by providing for us what we need to survive. He does not change our painful circumstances. He sustains us through them."[61]

~ Charles Stanley ~

It is really hard to make an ending to this book, because life just keeps on happening every day. It would be so easy to keep adding chapters. After what has happened in the past week, I could easily slip in another. This finale is to encourage you to hang on to the promises of God and know that He is ever faithful no matter what you may be going through, even if your trial lingers longer than you want it to. I love that great hymn, "Great Is Thy Faithfulness," written by Thomas Chisholm. Especially the part that says, "Morning by morning new mercies I see." Every day is a new day and we can learn something new from Him every day, if we let Him teach us. It is one of my top ten hymns. It has been one of my favorites since I was a little girl. I was raised in a small Pentecostal church where we sang all those beautiful hymns. The verse behind the song is found in Lamentations 3:22-24 "Through the Lord's mercies we are not consumed, because His compassions fail not. They are new every morning, great is Your faithfulness. 'The Lord is my portion,' says my soul, therefore I hope in Him!'"

Thomas Chisholm wrote this all-time inspiring hymn as a tribute to God's faithfulness through his very ordinary life. He became a Christian when he was twenty-seven and entered the ministry when he was thirty-six. His health was so poor that it forced him to retire after just one year. Though this was a disappointing chapter in his life, God was so faithful. Chisholm then took a job as a life insurance agent. He wrote nearly 1,200 poems throughout his life, including several hymns that were published. Toward the end of his life he said, "My income has not been large at any time due to impaired health in the earlier years which has followed me on until now. Although I must not fail to record here the unfailing faithfulness of a covenant-keeping God and that He has given me many wonderful displays of His providing care, for which I am filled with astonishing gratefulness."[62]

Great is Thy faithfulness,
Great is Thy faithfulness,
Morning by morning new mercies I see;
All I have needed Thy hand hath provided.[63]

God has truly been so faithful to me throughout my life! Has He given me everything I wanted? Absolutely not. But He has never left my side, even when I have doubted Him. I wish I could give you all the answers as to why God is not answering your prayer, at least not the way you want Him to. This is where faith comes in. This is where you make the choice to trust Him no matter what.

I think of the time Jesus was preaching to a group of people, and it was one of those hard sayings of His. Let me set the stage. John 6 is such an interesting chapter. We see in the first few verses Jesus performs one of His greatest miracles, the feeding of the 5,000. This miracle impresses the crowd so much that they wanted to make Jesus king, but instead, He withdrew to a mountain to spend time with His Father. He was not ready for Palm Sunday yet. In the meantime, His disciples were having a bit of trouble crossing the lake. When they just about reached the middle, a storm rose up. As they were struggling, Jesus comes to them walking on the water. At first they were frightened thinking He was a ghost.

How could that be? They nearly spent every day with Him. They just spent the afternoon with Him feeding the 5,000, yet they did not recognize Him. When Jesus convinced them that He was not a ghost, He got into the boat and took them to shore, and calmed the storm. The very next day some of that same crowd was looking for Jesus on the other side of the lake. They were probably looking for another miracle and another sign so that they could "see it and believe it." Did they forget what Jesus did the day before? Wasn't that enough? Obviously not! But instead of another miracle, they got this weird sermon.

Jesus said in John 6:54, "Whoever eats my flesh and drinks my blood has eternal life, and I will raise them up at the last day." Wow. This was not what they were looking for. Many turned from following Him that day because of what He said. They counted the cost and thought the cost was more than they could afford. And besides, what was Jesus talking about? It just did not make sense. John 6:60 says, "On hearing it, many of his disciples said, 'This is a hard teaching. Who can accept it?'" Instead of trusting Him or asking Him to explain it, they just left. Jesus did not preach to please His audience. If He did, He would have taken back everything He said when He noticed how everyone was reacting to it. I think it was more of a hard sermon to accept than a hard sermon to understand. Jesus was demanding complete allegiance to Him. No more playing games. No more miracles to keep them coming. He was asking for one hundred percent dedication! They were not ready to put their complete trust in Him, especially when they couldn't understand everything He was saying.

Do you ever feel that way? Do you ever say, "This is too hard!" What's the use? I am getting nowhere fast. I just don't understand what He wants from me. I don't think I can do it." Do you ever think about throwing in the towel and throwing your faith in with it?

I love the next few verses that really put it all into perspective and force you make a choice. John 6:66-68 says, "From this time many of his disciples turned back and no longer followed Him. 'You do not want to leave too, do you?' Jesus asked the Twelve. Simon Peter answered Him, 'Lord, to whom shall we go?'"

We do have a choice. We can let our situation cause us to be bitter and indifferent. And then what—walk away from God? Where else can we go? Or we can choose to put our faith and trust in a faithful God even though we don't quite understand it all. I can't imagine trying to do life without God. Though we can't understand it all now, someday we will see the whole picture, if we just hold on.

I started having a "poor me week" that has turned into a "poor me month." I will be starting a new regime of chemotherapy. My doctor in St. Louis thought it would be more convenient for me to do it where I live, instead of driving to St. Louis, which is a 1 ½ hour drive away, two days in a row, every week, indefinitely. Long story short, I got sick in between (that awful flu) so my major tests, including bone marrow biopsy and insertion of a port, have been put on hold. Not that I look forward to it, but it is like going to the dentist, just go and get it over with. I have had a lingering cough and fever which tend to wear a healthy person down. But I am amazed at how God works. He must outright laugh at me. God's timing is the right time.

There are days I look up to heaven and say, "Why me?" There are days I just literally cry out and say, "I cannot do this anymore! I do not want to do this anymore! I'm not going to do this anymore." But guess what? I am still here doing what I do not want to do and I am amazed at God's faithfulness. It is for sure new every morning. We never know what a day may bring but we always can know that He will be faithful. Unfortunately we have to keep on going. Too bad we are so human at times and want to quit. It really can cramp our style. But in the midst of the everyday feeling that you are drowning, God comes through, throwing you a life preserver and giving you a little bit of encouragement. I would rather have a bolt of His healing power go through my body and be instantly healed right this minute, but if not, then I will just let God prove His faithfulness. So this morning, this new morning, my daughter-in-law sends me a text to read a portion of scripture. She sent me this message with it:

January 22, 2014

You need to read Lamentations 3:20-42. It is appropriate for you, too. This was God's message to me today, and then I looked up from my Bible and the sun was shining and it was snowing. Just now, for a little bit, then it stopped. I needed that.

Is it not amazing what each of us needs to be uplifted? It was sunshine and snow for my daughter-in-law. Just seeing God in the little everyday occurrences that we might miss. And any other day she might have missed it, trying to take care of my three energetic grandchildren, ages five, four, and one, but not today. Why? Last night she was rushed to the emergency room, by ambulance, because she had a severe asthma attack. I am not wishing anyone to be sick, but I can tell you that when your life passes before you, you have a new appreciation for the simple things in life. For life itself. She told me she thought she was "going to see Jesus." I am so glad she did not.

This chapter of Lamentations is so good. Although this book is filled with a weeping prophet crying out to God over the condition of the children of Israel, it is filled with hope and assurance of God's faithfulness to an unfaithful people. Aren't we all like that at times?

"I remember my affliction and my wandering, the bitterness and the gall. I well remember them, and my soul is downcast within me. Yet this I call to mind and therefore I have hope: Because of the Lord's great love we are not consumed, for his compassions never fail. They are new every morning; great is Your faithfulness. I say to myself, 'The Lord is my portion; therefore I will wait for Him.' The Lord is good to those whose hope is in Him, to the one who seeks Him; it is good to wait quietly for the salvation of the Lord. It is good for a man to bear the yoke while he is young. Let him sit alone in silence, for the Lord has laid it on him. Let him bury his face in the dust— there may yet be hope. Let him offer his cheek to one who would strike him, and let him be filled with disgrace. For no one is cast off by the Lord forever. Though He brings grief, He will show compassion, so great is his unfailing love. For He does not willingly bring affliction or grief to anyone." Lamentations 3:19-33

I like what Chuck Smith says about this portion of scripture. "Jeremiah related his depth of despair and hopelessness over his calamities. And hopelessness always leads to depression, (*Especially when we allow it to*). Jeremiah was at one of the lowest points of his life. But all of a sudden there is a dramatic change as Jeremiah adjusts his thinking (*in other words he gets an "attitude adjustment"*). We can think ourselves into hopelessness and despair, or by the renewing of our mind we can come into a whole new state of consciousness of God to attain victory and hope."[64] Amen!

Ephesians 4:23 says: ". . . to be made new in the attitude of your minds . . . "II Corinthians

10:5 says: ". . . we take captive every thought to make it obedient to Christ." Isaiah 26:3 says: "You will keep in perfect peace those whose minds are steadfast, because they trust in you."

It is such an amazing feeling when you can share spiritual truths with your adult children. It made me cry. It does not take much these days. Then she texted me this: "Maybe only to verse 33, the rest is Israel's captivity." I texted back: "OK. I don't want to be a captive."

At this point Paul Harvey would say, "And now the rest of the story." About fifteen minutes before Melanie's text, my friend Chris sent me a text with a Bible verse. Can you guess what the verse was? Lamentations 3:24-26. Could this be a coincidence? Guess you can say that. But I choose to believe it was a God moment giving me a bit of hope in a hopeless situation, and the Creator of life reminding me that He is faithful. Always has and always will be.

P.S
Heaven Is For Real

I pray that this book has helped to encourage you as you face your most difficult challenges in life. Most of all I hope this book has helped you realize that there is only one true source of strength that can fill the empty places in your heart and help you climb your most challenging mountain. It would be negligence on my part if I did not offer you the free gift that God wants to give everyone who will accept it. Romans 6:23 says, "For the wages of sin is death, but the gift of God is eternal life in Christ Jesus our Lord." If you have never asked Jesus to come into your heart to be your Lord and Savior, I pray you will do it now. None of us are guaranteed tomorrow. Hebrews 4:16 says, "Let us then approach God's throne of grace with confidence, so that we may receive mercy and find grace to help us in our time of need." Jesus is only a prayer away.

There is a movie that recently came out called, "Heaven Is For Real." I hear it was a very inspiring film. But I have known heaven was for real for a long time. Jesus promised each one of us in John 14:3, "And if I go and prepare a place for you, I will come back and take you to be with me that you also may be where I am." Heaven is for real and Jesus is preparing a place for those who will accept Him.

There was an experience I had with one of our prayer teams, during one of our praise and worship times at my house. Several of us were gathered in my living room listening to praise and worship music and inviting God's presence. I had my hands raised and eyes closed worshipping God like everyone else. Suddenly I noticed the music was fading and I was no longer in my living room. I saw a long stairway going up into the clouds and I knew where it was going. I was filled with joy as I leaped up those steps. I felt like I was floating.

It was bright yet hazy, and nothing was really focused. When I got to the top I saw a man in a white robe sitting on a throne with His arms outstretched to me smiling. His face was not clear but as I ran into His arms His hug was for real. As we embraced I felt so alive and happy but immediately He turned me around and gave me a gentle push to go back down the stairs. I did not hesitate and leaped down the stairs as happy as I went up them. The scene changed and I was in a hospital bed with my husband beside me. When I opened my eyes I looked at him and immediately grasped his hand, as we hurried out of the room. Suddenly the scene changed and I started hearing praise and worship music again. I opened my eyes and there I was in my living room. I looked around. Everyone was in their places praising and worshipping the Lord. No one knew anything happened and I was speechless. I kept this to myself. Did I leave my body and go to heaven? I don't think so. Whatever I experienced and however God did it, I felt He was again telling me heaven is for real and that He was not quite finished with me yet.

If you are breathing, God is not finished with you yet. Find out what He wants you to do. He will give you the strength you need to do it. I am living proof of that. Don't let anyone or anything separate you from the love He wants to pour out on you. If you are struggling, know that God is there to help you. He will do amazing things in your life, if you will allow Him to.

Thank you for sharing your time with me and remember, "If your mountain won't move, climb it!"

~Annette Whitmire~

Endnotes

Introduction

[1] thinkexixt.com

[2] wikipedia.org

Chapter 1

[3] lifeloveandfamily.net

[4] achieveyourlifemission.com © Copyright Randal Wright 2011 - 2014

[5] National Women's Day magazine of The National Women's Day Department of the Assemblies of God 2012. Thoughts used by permission.

[6] gismocrazed.com

Chapter 2

[7] searchquotes.com

[8] mcdc.missouri.edu

Chapter 3

[9] Used by permission from TDJ enterprises ©2014

[10] blueletterbible.org/Lexicon :: Strong's G4624

Chapter 4

[11] izquotes.com

[12] kididdles.com/anonymous

Chapter 5
[13] cancerhawk.com

[14] youtube.com

Chapter 6
[15] thinkexist.com

[16] quotes.net

Chapter 7
[17] brainyquote.com

[18] songlyrics.com

[19] "God Will Make A Way" by Don Moen. EMI Christian Music. Used by permission.

Chapter 8
[20] brainyquote.com

[21] searchquotes.com/author unknown

[22] blueletterbible.org/Lexicon :: Strong's G3398

[23] christiananswers.net

[24] lyrics.time

Chapter 9
[25] Used by permission. Great Day Every Day by Max Lucado, 2011, Thomas Nelson. Nashville, Tennessee. All rights reserved.

Chapter 10
[26] wikipedia.org

Chapter 11
[27] quoteswise.com

Chapter 12
[28] izquotes.com

[29] answers.ask.com

[30] ehow.com

[31] md anderson.org

[32] cancer.org

Chapter 13
[33] thinkexist.com

[34] ©2009-2014 Joni and Friends - All Rights Reserved. Used by permission.

Chapter 15
[35] searchquotes.com

[36] metrolyrics.com

[37] ezinearticles.com

Chapter 16
[38] thinkexist.com

[39] searchquotes.com/quotes/author/Ambrose Redmoon

[40] brainyquote.com

[41] Dr. Kevin D. Glen, Memorial Baptist Church. Used by permission.

Chapter 17
[42] brainyquote.com

[43] newsboys.com

[44] merriam-webster.com

[45] Secretary of the Treasury, Mr. William Lowndes (1652-1724) /izquotes.com

[46] azlyrics.com

Chapter 18
[47] thinkexist.com

[48] searchquotes.com

[49] blueletterbible.org/Lexicon :: Strong's G3986

[50] dictionary.com

[51] goodreads.com

[52] businessdictionary.com

Chapter 19

[53] goodreads.com

[54] praisejesustoday.com

[55] Permission to use lyrics from Mark Bishop's Can I Pray For You provided courtesy of Mark Bishop, Centergy Music, Possum Run Music and Sonlite Records.

Chapter 20

[56] goodreads.com

[57] © 2010 Warren W Wiersbe. Be Strong (Joshua): Putting God's Power to Work in Your Life is published by David C Cook. All rights reserved. Used by permission.

[58] blueletterbible.org/Lexicon :: Strong's G3874

[59] ©2012 Gail McWilliams. Seeing Beyond: Choosing To Look Past the Horizon. Used by permission. gailmcwillaims.com

[60] Ibid.

Chapter 21

[61] Used by permission. How to Handle Adversity, Charles Stanley, 1989, Thomas Nelson. Nashville, Tennessee. All rights reserved.

Chapter 21

[62] gaither.com

[63] ibid

[64] blueletterbible.org/Chuck Smith study guide for Lamentations.